Cajus Bekker

THE GERMAN NAVY
1939-1945

Hamlyn
London · New York · Sydney · Toronto

© 1972 Gerhard Stalling Verlag,
Oldenburg und Hamburg
English translation © 1974 The Hamlyn Publishing Group Limited
London · New York · Sydney · Toronto
Astronaut House, Feltham, Middlesex, England

Printed in Great Britain by
Butler & Tanner Limited, Frome and London

ISBN 0 600 37059 3

Illustration acknowledgments
Author's collection (48), Bibliothek für Zeitgeschichte (22),
Bundesarchiv (5), B. Drüppel (9), Archiv W. Freese (8), E. Gröner
(ship drawings), E. de Jong (8), A. Mitbauer (1), W. Schöppe (12),
Ullstein Bildarchiv (22), F. Urbahns (39).
The remaining illustrations are from private collections.
The maps were drawn by Werner Schmidt.

Contents

Foreword

Roughly three decades have gone by since the Second World War held the world in its grip and brought suffering to millions of people. Today, in the face of new world problems, the events and personalities of this fateful period have already become history. Not that they have been forgotten—on the contrary, they arouse a great deal of interest not only among those who took part in the war, but even more so among the young generation, eager to learn what really happened.

Such interest is natural in a country with Great Britain's strong naval tradition, and in the years since the War it has produced a flow of books about naval strategy in the War, and about the Royal Navy and its part in the victory. But in defeated Germany it was bound to develop much more slowly, for the deeply disillusioned war generation had no deisre to hear anything more about it.

The younger generation, however, especially those born after 1945, naturally felt no sense of responsibility or guilt for Hitler's Germany and the War, and instead nourished a healthy curiosity about it.

If a book is to satisfy this curiosity, this desire for the facts, it must obviously avoid stereotypes and clichés, the black-and-white simplicity of heroes and cowards that wartime propaganda breeds and that even now leaves its traces. What is needed instead is an objective account, based on historical fact, of the background of the War's events and their inter-relationships, in recognition of the fact that no mistakes or failures can be covered up if the story is to hold water and cast events in their true light.

It is with this principle in mind that this book has been written and assembled. What places it ahead of the many other picture books of German warships is not only the exceptionally high quality of the photographs, but also its layout and organization as a compact, lucid and comprehensive account of the war at sea in word and picture. In creating it the author has relied on the fruits of his research, which have appeared previously in his other books on the air and sea war, all of them translated into many languages.

Thus the following pages describe the building up of the German fleet from scratch during the 20s; the construction of the pocket battleships, which caused a world sensation; Germany's flaunting of the dictates of the Treaty of Versailles; and the grand plans for the new German naval might that culminated in the 1939 Z-Plan—and that, a few months later, were disrupted by the unexpected outbreak of war.

The German Navy had to confront her old and new enemy, England, with only half a fleet. But instead of recognizing the potential of the U-boat arm and therefore concentrating efforts on building it up, the German Naval Staff expected a decisive success from the Navy's surface forces. The brief blossoming and collapse of this oceanic supply campaign, the imprisonment of the main force in the Arctic ocean, the loss of the big ships and of the U-boats' battle for the Atlantic—these are some of the important episodes described in the book. Nor should we neglect the struggles of the many flotillas of small German ships in European coastal waters right up to the 1944 invasion, and the flight across the Baltic in 1945, Germany's Dunkirk, which saved two million people from falling into Russian hands just before the collapse.

Cajus Bekker

Hamburg, December 1973

For a total of fourteen years and four months Dr Erich Raeder commanded the German Navy, becoming Grand Admiral on 1 April 1939. The building-up of the Navy was his work, and the officers in particular bore the stamp of his teachings. Raeder, son of a head-master, was born on 24 April 1876 and joined the Kaiser's Navy at the age of 18. In the First World War he was, as first staff officer, right-hand man of von Hipper, Flag Officer cruisers, and after the defeat of 1918 became Head of a Department in the new Admiralty. The events of the Kapp-Lüttwitz putsch, in which Raeder became unwittingly in-volved, and which he called a 'criminal step', strengthened his determination to give his unconditional loyalty to the elected government and the state. This was not the least of the reasons why, on 1 October 1928, he succeeded Admiral Zenker as Commander-in-Chief of the Navy. This position he retained under Hitler until his resignation at the beginning of 1943.

The Peacetime Build-up

It was 1920: the First World War had been lost, the Kaiser's Empire shattered; the Second Reich, the Weimar Republic, was established. Oddly, the victorious powers had not insisted on a complete demilitarization, but had restricted the Reich's armed forces to 100,000 men, which were to include a Navy with a maximum of 15,000 regulars.

The Treaty of Versailles had in fact placed severe restrictions on the Navy. Under Article 181 it was to contain not more than six armoured ships, six cruisers, twelve destroyers, and twelve torpedo boats, or the same number of replacements. All other existing warships were to be placed in reserve or converted into merchant ships. The construction or acquisition of submarines was forbidden, as was the possession of any military aircraft.

Article 190 of the Treaty of Versailles also regulated the replacement of obsolete ships. The terms dictated that, unless sunk or otherwise lost, battleships and cruisers could only be replaced after twenty years service, and destroyers and torpedo boats after fifteen. When new ships were built as replacements, 'battleships' would not have a displacement of over 10,000 tons, cruisers 6,000 tons, destroyers 800 tons, and torpedo boats 200 tons.

The reconstruction of the Navy was further complicated by the fact that the High Seas Fleet of the First World War, interned at the end of the war in Scapa Flow, had been scuttled; and five 5,000-ton cruisers, only six to eight years old, and therefore comparatively modern, had to be handed over to the victorious powers as war reparations.

In the event the Navy brought into service a few light cruisers of the *Gazelle* class, built around the turn of the century, together with some old torpedo boats, and finally the veteran ships of the line. *Hannover* and *Braunschweig*, followed in 1924 by *Elsass* and *Hessen*, and later by the necessarily modernized *Schlesien* and *Schleswig-Holstein* (see page 14), the only ships of their class that were to survive the Second World War as well as the First.

Naturally, attention was focused on the first new ships to be built,

The German Navy resumed service in 1920–21 with a dozen old torpedo boats, all built before the First World War. This one is *T157*, which was still serving in the Baltic as a torpedo recovery boat twenty years later, till she hit a mine in the Bay of Danzig on 22 October 1943.

especially on the third cruiser, bearing the traditional name *Emden*, whose construction had been commissioned and begun in 1921, but whose completion was delayed by political and financial difficulties. When the *Emden* was finally launched on 7 January 1925, going into service the same year, the first step towards the creation of a new Navy had been taken. With her eight 5.9-inch guns in single mountings, she was modelled on the last light cruisers built in the war. The Navy was as yet forbidden to develop new guns—particularly in twin or triple gun turrets—though later this and other restrictions were successfully ignored. Thus the *Emden* remained the only ship of its type; subsequent light cruisers of the *K*-class embodied a large number of improvements.

From 1925 there began to appear on the slipways of the naval shipyard at Wilhelmshaven the first new torpedo boats, classified under the Treaty of Versailles as 'destroyers'. These were the boats of the *Raubvogel* (bird of prey) and *Raubtier* (beast of prey) class, whose displacement was not the 800 tons prescribed by the Treaty but 930 tons. Here too the shipbuilders made good use of the experience they had gained from the wartime torpedo boats. These boats—except for the *Tiger*, rammed and sunk by the destroyer *Max Schultz* on 25 August 1939 in the Baltic—

Another boat from the early days, the *T111*, which was in fact the torpedo boat *G11* built in the Germania shipyard in Kiel in 1913. Boats of this type displaced 570 tons, could steam at 33 knots and were armed with two 3.5-inch guns and four torpedo tubes. Towards the end of the twenty years more and more of them were replaced by the new *Möwe* class boats, but they stayed in service for many years as auxiliary craft.

9

survived arduous duties throughout the Second World War right up to the struggle against the invasion forces in June 1944. The five-strong torpedo boat flotilla based at Le Havre, under the command of Lieutenant-Commander Heinrich Hoffmann, put out against the mighty invasion fleet with the boats *Möwe*, *Falke* and *Jaguar*. The Allies responded with a devastating bombing raid on Le Havre, sinking the last remaining boats of the *Raubtier* and *Raubvogel* class.

The first entirely new ships came in the years 1926–30, and these were the three *K*-class cruisers *Königsberg*, *Karlsruhe* and *Köln.* They displaced 6,650 tons, and were the first to have a director fire control for their nine

The first twelve new torpedo boats built by the Navy were named after birds and animals of prey. On the left, from top to bottom, are *Greif*, *Wolf* and *Kondor*, on manoeuvres. Above is *Falke* with a flotilla. These boats displaced 930 tons, could steam at 33 knots, had 122-man crews and carried six torpedo tubes as well as three 4.1-inch guns or three 5-inch guns in single mountings. Certainly they could not be called destroyers, but they were a big step forward.

The Navy's first new ship: the light cruiser *Emden*, completed in 1925, which in memory of the famous raider of the First War bore an Iron Cross on her bows. The *Emden* (top)—as she looked when completed—was used principally as a training ship and took many cadets on voyages round the world.

5.9-inch guns, mounted in triple turrets; their engine-room installation also justified their claim to be the world's most modern light cruisers. Besides the main turbines they were equipped with twin diesels for cruising which consumed fuel at a much reduced rate. This was a development which was to arouse worldwide attention when applied to another type of ship to be built by the new German Navy.

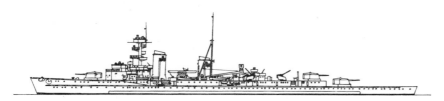

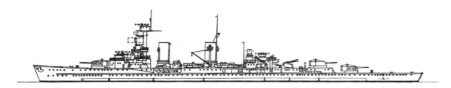

In order to accelerate her completion, *Emden* (top drawing) carried eight 5.9-inch guns in obsolete single mountings. Her displacement was 5,600 tons, and her two BBC turbines, producing 46,500 h.p., gave her a speed of 29 knots. Her crew numbered 636, including 162 cadets, and she carried anti-aircraft guns as well as four torpedo tubes. Considerable improvements were incorporated in the three *K*-cruisers that left the yards in 1927 and 1928. *Karlsruhe* (middle drawing), *Köln* and *Königsberg* (bottom drawing) displaced 6,650 tons and were 560 feet long, with a beam of 50 feet and a draught of 18 feet. Two turbines producing 65,000 h.p. were teamed with twin cruising diesels yielding 18,000 h.p. Top speed was 32 knots. Armament consisted of nine 5.9-inch guns in triple turrets, six 3.5-inch and eight 37 mm anti-aircraft guns, all in twin mountings, as well as various 20 mm AA guns, twelve torpedo tubes, a catapult and two aircraft.

Below is the *Königsberg*, sunk on 10 April 1940 by British dive bombers in Bergen harbour.

The Pocket Battleships

Under the restrictions imposed by the Treaty of Versailles, cruisers and torpedo boats could still be built, but what were the prospects for the replacement of the elderly and now totally obsolete battleships? At the end of the 20s the Navy was still putting to sea in the veteran battleships of the *Deutschland* class, built between 1903 and 1908, which were no match for a modern battleship either in armour, or armament. In the Washington naval agreement of 1922 Great Britain, France, Italy, Japan and the United States had agreed to limit the size of their own capital ships to 35,000 tons, and their heavy guns to a calibre of 16 inches. For Germany, however, a different set of restrictions was applied: replacement 'battleships', if they could so be called, were not to exceed a displacement of 10,000 tons. The intention was clear enough. The German fleet would be able to fulfil a limited role protecting Germany's shores, but the world's sea powers would have nothing to fear from it. Yet from the drawing boards of Germany's naval constructors came some astounding suggestions. Basically the following alternatives were available: either one could build a slow coastal warship, well armoured against fire from land and suitable for instance for safeguarding seaborne trade with the Eastern provinces of the Reich, cut off by Poland; or one could aim for

something completely new in warship design, a ship halfway between a cruiser and a battleship, not as fast as the cruisers of the sea powers, but more heavily armoured and armed—not as heavily armed as the battleships but faster than them so that it could avoid a battle with a superior opponent.

Thus an excellent solution was evolved: a ship no bigger than the so-called 'Washington cruiser', the 10,000-ton heavy cruiser with 8-inch guns that all the sea powers were building, yet a ship that would have nothing to fear from the Washington cruiser, for it would have heavier, 11-inch guns, with a longer range, and in turn would be better armed against the lighter 8-inch guns.

However, the German Navy then had a man bitterly opposed to the concept of the pocket battleship, though later, in the Second World War, he needed them urgently for his own naval strategy. The man was Admiral Erich Raeder. At this time, as chief of the Baltic Station, he favoured the slow coastal warship, which would certainly have been more suitable for operations in the Baltic—against Russia or Poland. In the 20s no one had the slightest notion of the new worldwide naval war that was to take place. Yet the Navy opted for the new pocket battleship with its unique attributes, and when Raeder himself took over command of the Navy in Berlin on 1 October 1928, he made no alterations to it. He defended the plan against severe opposition in the Reichstag and soon the world discovered what the German warship-builders had been up to. It was a shock. A small selection of quotes from the 30s bears witness to the excitement, apprehension and even unbounded admiration of naval experts in the face of this new weapon. On 9 January 1930 *Shipbuilding and Shipping Record* stated

The first ship to be launched as a replacement for obsolete battleships like the 1908-built *Schlesien* (opposite) was the *Deutschland* (above) launched on 19 May 1931 and commissioned on 1 April 1933. The ship, constructed with the limits imposed by the Treaty of Versailles in mind, aroused worldwide attention because, theoretically, it was more powerful than faster ships of other nations and faster than their more powerful ones.

Dressed overall and crew lining the ship's side—the second of the pocket battleships, *Admiral Scheer*, ahead of the first, the *Deutschland*. Their six 11-inch guns and massive build earned them the 'pocket battleship' tag.

that the 10,000-ton Washington cruiser, whose value had already been doubted in many quarters, was hopeless by comparison with the German 10,000-ton pocket battleship. In its 8 January 1930 issue *Naval and Military Record* hailed the ship as the pacesetter for a reduction in the size of battleships. It pointed out that in strategic and tactical terms it made a point that could not possibly be allowed to pass unobserved. Germany had clearly shown the world that the huge increase in the size of battleships was totally fruitless and that size had little to do with fighting capability. In the same journal, on 22 January 1930, Sir Herbert Russell asserted that the new German ship represented the warship of the future; a ship of this type combined the qualities of a battleship with the versatility of a cruiser. This was vital, for the battleship of the future needed to be able to undertake the widest possible range of tasks.

Again and again the new German ship was compared with the other seapowers' heavy cruisers of the same tonnage. The May issue of *U.S. Naval Institute Proceedings* maintained that the ship, with its six 11-inch and eight 5.9-inch guns, together with armour capable of withstanding 8-inch shells, could justifiably be hailed as the most powerful 10,000-ton ship ever built. It was not a substitute for the present type of Washington cruiser, for it had the capability to outfight the Washington cruiser if the latter was forced to do battle. It went on to say that the Germans had problems to deal with which were different from those of the U.S. Navy and which they had, with this new creation, most admirably mastered.

Admiral Scheer, commissioned in November 1934, was the most successful ship of its class in the war.

18

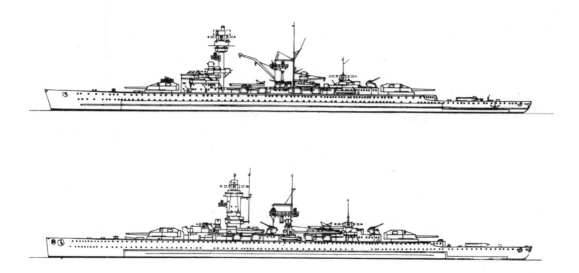

Soon, especially in Paris, a counterpoise was being advocated. This is what *Le Temps* of Paris had to say on 5 September 1930: 'Germany has taken the lead with a battleship whose technical specification is first class. Those who talked of the abolition of battleships spoke too soon. It is now up to the victorious powers to follow Germany's example—indeed they are compelled to do so.' The French answer was to build the two battle-cruisers *Dunkerque* and *Strasbourg*, which were faster and more powerful than the German pocket battleships—and which in these respects were only matched by the British battle-cruisers *Hood*, *Repulse* and *Renown*.

The British remained calmer. Even if five more pocket battleships were built, said *The Times* of 19 February 1930, the German fleet would still be inferior to that of each of the seapowers in the London Treaty. And that hit the nail on the head.

Berlin was flattered and encouraged by the reaction of the sea powers. 'Panzerschiff A', reads an internal memorandum, 'is evidently causing some disquiet to the powers involved in the Washington agreement, for it represents in their eyes a new type of ship which does not fall within the categories laid down . . .' Yet objections could not be justified, for 'Our *Panzerschiff* conforms precisely with the terms of the Versailles Treaty. These stipulations were not made by us, nor even arrived at with our collaboration, but were simply imposed on us by the other powers, who now find themselves so discomfited by the end product of these very restrictions. Regarding the latter, the preamble to Part V of the Treaty states that Germany is duty bound not to overstep them, "in order to facilitate the introduction of a general restriction of armaments on the part of all nations . . ." Germany has shown just how much striking power can be embodied in a 10,000-ton ship; thus it should be seen as representing a step towards disarmament rather than a hindrance to disarmament . . .'

The pocket battleship *Deutschland* (top drawing), built in the years 1929–33 in the Deutsche Werke Kiel, displaced 11,700 tons, measured 609 feet over-all, with a beam of 67·5 feet, and drew 21·6 feet. Eight diesels developing 54,000 h.p. gave her a maximum speed of 26 knots. Even at high speeds range was 10,000 nautical miles, while at lower speeds it was even greater. Armament consisted of six 11-inch guns in triple turrets, eight 5.9-inch, six 4.1-inch AA guns and eight 37 mm AA guns in twin mountings, numerous 20 mm AA guns, eight torpedo tubes and two aircraft.

Admiral Graf Spee (lower drawing) and the (till her conversion) very similar *Admiral Scheer* displaced 12,100 tons, and, though differing in some details, carried the same armament.

On the opposite page are seen the three pocket battleships in March 1939. *Admiral Scheer* (middle picture) was modified during the first winter of the war, receiving a slender fighting top in place of its massive control tower.

The Light Cruisers *Leipzig* and *Nürnberg*

The last two light cruisers built in Germany, *Leipzig* and *Nürnberg*, commissioned in 1931 and 1935 respectively, differed from their predecessors the *K*-class cruisers in that they had only one funnel and in that their after triple 5.9-inch gun turrets were positioned on the centre line. The power installation was also considerably improved: Four MAN two-stroke diesels producing 12,400 h.p. were coupled to a third screw providing the cruisers with a cruising speed of 18 knots independent of the main turbines. *Leipzig* and *Nürnberg* formed part of the Navy's reconnaissance forces. On 13 December 1939 they steamed with the cruiser *Köln* out into the North Sea, under the command of Rear Admiral Günther Lütjens. Their mission was to make contact with five destroyers returning from a minelaying operation off the English coast and give them protection on the homeward run. However, the cruisers were sighted by the British submarine *Salmon*. At 11.24 hours the *Leipzig*, and three minutes later the *Nürnberg*, were hit by torpedoes. The destroyers then took up position to protect the cruisers against further attack. Both ships reached harbour and were repaired, though the *Leipzig* had been so badly damaged that she was afterwards used only as a training ship.

Both these cruisers survived the war, although the *Leipzig* was rammed amidships by the heavy cruiser *Prinz Eugen* in fog in the Gulf of Danzig in October 1944 (see page 188). The *Nürnberg* was taken to Libau at the beginning of January 1946, and was still serving in 1961 under the Soviet flag as the *Admiral Makarow*.

'The German 6,000-ton cruisers are convincing proof of the Germans' ability to produce the maximum fighting power from a given displacement,' said British naval experts in the 30s. At the beginning of the war the *Leipzig* (below) was so badly hit by a torpedo from a British submarine that she could only thenceforth be used as a training ship.

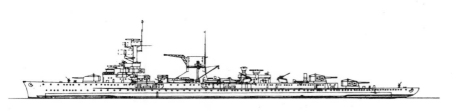

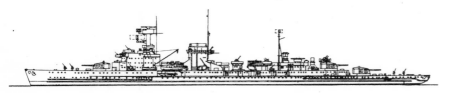

The *Nürnberg*, youngest and most modern of the German Navy's 6,000-ton cruisers, carried out extensive convoy and mining duties during the war, being handed over to the USSR after the surrender. Both the light cruisers *Leipzig* (6,515 tons, 580 feet overall, 850-man crew) and *Nürnberg (6,520* tons, 593 feet overall, 900-man crew) had 60,000-h.p. turbines giving a 32-knot maximum speed, as well as diesels. Their armament consisted of nine 5.9-inch guns in triple turrets, six to eight 3.5-inch and eight 37 mm AA guns, with a number of 20 mm AA guns, twelve torpedo tubes (the latter reduced during the war, and the *Leipzig*'s removed altogether), and two aircraft.

Signal flags drying out on the line on the cruiser *Köln*, while the forward funnel is being prepared for a new coat of paint.

The light cruiser *Königsberg* dwarfed by the cliffs of a Norwegian fjord. Among other duties, the cruisers served as training ships, including the traditional foreign cruises, as shown here.

The climax of a young officer cadet's career was the round-the-world voyage aboard a training ship. Here the cruiser *Karlsruhe* is leaving Kiel, flying the old naval ensign at the stern. The sail training ship *Gorch Fock* is accompanying the cruiser out into the Baltic. The voyage will take the ship round the Cape of Good Hope to Sumatra, Hong Kong and Japan. On the homeward voyage the *Karlsruhe* will pass through the Panama Canal and will drop anchor in Kiel again nine months later.

The New Destroyer Force

According to the stipulations laid down by the Treaty of Versailles German 'destroyers' should not exceed 800 tons. Yet the twelve boats of the *Raubvogel* and *Raubtier* class produced to meet this restriction were really only torpedo boats. So it is hardly surprising that at the beginning of the 30s there was a strong movement to build larger destroyers proper along the same lines as those of the other powers. Initially the size talked of was around 1,600 tons, but when the first destroyer was being built in the Kiel shipyards in 1934–35, estimates had grown to 2,232 tons, almost as big as a small cruiser before the First World War.

Experienced sailors immediately complained that the builders of this type of destroyer had given it a forecastle which turned out to be much too short. In fact sea trials showed that *Z1 Leberecht Maas* shipped so much water, even in a medium sea in the Baltic, that the forward gun could not be used at all and even those on the bridge were completely soaked. In spite of subsequent modifications this major problem remained, that German destroyers could not be classed as adequately seaworthy.

There were troubles, too, with the superheated steam installation, whose twin turbines were fed by six water-tube boilers giving 1,000 lb. per sq. in. (and in the 1934 type 1,650 lb. per sq. in.). Numerous tube fractures and other teething troubles were suffered, which added a further element of risk, particularly on operational sorties. In fact, the turbines developed 70,000 h.p. and under favourable conditions gave the ships a speed of 38 knots.

By September 1939, 22 destroyers had been commissioned, and in the first winter of the war the destroyer force, in spite of the handicaps that afflicted it, carried out secret operations which the enemy had thought impossible. Under cover of night they laid minefields in the estuaries and shipping lanes of the east coast of England, and the Royal Navy, unaware of this danger, lost a number of ships as a result.

Z1 Leberecht Maass (opposite, top) and *Z16 Friedrich Eckoldt* (opposite, middle) were respectively the first and last boats of the 1934 class destroyer. *Z21 Wilhelm Heidkamp* (below) was the ship of Captain 'D', or Captain Destroyers Commodore Bonte, and, like *Z20 Karl Galster* (opposite bottom) was of the 1936 class. All the destroyers built before the war had five 5-inch guns, as well as AA guns and eight torpedo tubes. They were also equipped to lay 60 mines.

U-boats from Scratch

It looked as if the German Navy would have to start absolutely from scratch, as far as submarines were concerned, when Hitler, on 16 March 1935, proclaimed Germany's military independence. He ignored the ban on U-boat building and, three months later, concluded a naval treaty with the British enabling him to build U-boat tonnage up to 45 per cent of the Royal Navy's. The heads of the German Navy in the Second Republic had, however, never lost sight of the possibility that this day might come, and had made extensive provisions for it. Their aim was to ensure that Germany should not neglect U-boat design, and they had consequently set up a private German-controlled ship construction and design office on Dutch territory, which soon got its first orders.

From German plans, but in Dutch, Spanish and Finnish shipyards, a number of U-boats were built, including the small Finnish *Vesikko* and the big Turkish *Gür*, whose blueprints were soon ready once the command was given to put together a new German U-boat force. The *Vesikko* in particular soon had a number of successors, for it was from her that the German U-boat Type II was developed. Through secret prefabrication, 24 U-boats were built in little more than 12 months, and by autumn 1936 they had all been commissioned. These were small coastal U-boats of just over 250 tons displacement, and were christened 'canoes' by their 25-man crews. They had only three torpedo tubes with only one spare torpedo for each tube, and because of this and their limited range they were unsuitable for large-scale operations.

Yet it was these small boats, whose crews were trained by Hitler's

The first 'canoes', *U1* to *U6*, were built in record time in 1935. Their successors *U7* to *U23* were completed equally rapidly, and, with nearly double the fuel capacity, were able to stay at sea much longer. These Type II and IIa boats, displacing something between 254 and 279 tons, were suitable because of their small size only for service in coastal waters. From 1940, therefore, they were mostly used for training new U-boat crews.

newly-appointed U-boat chief Captain Karl Dönitz, and with which Dönitz evolved his later 'wolf-pack' tactics, that only six years later made their mark on the bitter struggle for the Atlantic. Dönitz was certain that in a new war the British would not send their merchant shipping out unprotected, but rather would safeguard them in heavily protected convoys. He foresaw only one way of overcoming this: if the enemy were to concentrate his shipping in convoys, he would send concentrations of U-boats into their midst.

It soon became clear that the type best suited for this sort of warfare, ranging over large areas of sea, would be a U-boat of medium size and great endurance, yet manoeuvrable enough to meet the rapidly changing situations of the actual battle. This, the Type VII, was in fact already available, but far too few had been built, and despite all the appeals and representations made by the head of the U-boat arm, the naval high command insisted that very large and expensive U-boats were also required for overseas operations in a properly balanced fleet.

When war broke out in September 1939, the German Navy had at its disposal 57 U-boats, of which only 26 were suitable for an Atlantic campaign against England. Germany's recognition of her inadequate strength in this respect overshadowed all the individual U-boat successes of the early years of the war, and by the time the deficiency was made up, it was too late, for by then the enemy had built up his defences and knew how to protect himself against attacks on his vital lifelines.

The two 862-ton *U25* and *U26* were the only boats of their class, developed from a prototype built in Spain from German plans and which later became the Turkish *Gür*. Another U-boat design, Type III, was better suited for an Atlantic campaign. *U26* was destroyed by British depth charges on 1 July 1940, while *U25* sank after hitting a mine a month later.

The major burden of the battle for the Atlantic fell on the Type VII U-boat. It was developed from the reliable Second World War UBIII Type and was substantially improved after 1939. Altogether 691 boats were built, from the pre-war Type VIIa (left) of 626 tons to the well-tried Type VIIc of 761 tons. They had five torpedo tubes and carried various other weapons during the war for use against seaborne targets as well as for protection against air attacks.

Parades in front of the Commander-in-Chief of the Navy were viewed with sarcasm by young U-boat officers, for their opinions on the ideal U-boat building programme were not shared by the high command in Berlin. In September 1939 only a handful of boats were available to fight against Britain.

The Naval Air Arm

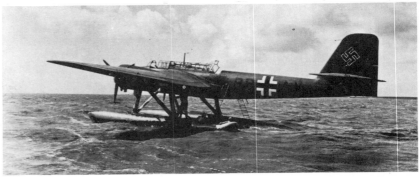

In the 30s the Navy recognized the need to build up a naval airarm, but Goering's motto, 'Everything that flies belongs to me,' put paid to this plan. Naval airmen remained the poor relatives of the Luftwaffe, largely cut off from the trend towards more powerful and faster aircraft. On the right are shown the Do.18 flying boat, a slow and vulnerable long-range marine reconnaissance aircraft, and below it the He.115, used among other things as a torpedo-carrying aircraft. It too was markedly inferior to enemy fighters.

The seaplanes and flying boats flown over the seas by the Luftwaffe were more cumbersome than land-based aircraft used over the seas and therefore no match for them. Here are shown the old Heinkel He.59 'double-decker' already used in the Spanish Civil War (left), later as minelayers and rescue aircraft, and (below) the short-range reconnaissance He.60 of the Holtenau squadron, as carried in the cruiser *Nürnberg*.

The Battleships *Gneisenau* and *Scharnhorst*

The *Gneisenau*, built by Deutsche Werke Kiel, served as fleet flagship and, in company with her sister-ship *Scharnhorst*, carried out a number of daring missions. Her end was typical: in 1942, after the lucky Channel breakthrough, she was knocked out by a severe hit from a bomb.

'Talk only about improved 10,000-ton ships but never mention 26,000 tons.' This was Hitler's order to his Navy chief Raeder in a conversation in June 1934. He was speaking of the two new ships of the *Deutschland* class now on the stocks, which were being considerably enlarged actually during construction. Both ships were first of all given a much stronger armour protection, while the power installation was changed to turbines, as the diesels developed for the *Deutschland* class developed insufficient power for ships of nearly three times the *Deutschland*'s displacement.

In the event, the *Gneisenau* and the *Scharnhorst*, though later always described as being of 26,000 tons, both displaced 31,850 tons. Thus they would by international standards have been full battleships, but for the fact that their main armament had been kept to 11 inches. There was talk of replacing these with 15-inch guns, but after two years delay the Navy, faced with the worsening situation in the second half of the 30s, was unable to carry out the work. Thus there came into existence two fast and modern ships, similar to battle-cruisers, yet unable through inferiority of firepower to stand up to the heavy ships of the enemy.

The *Scharnhorst*, built in the Navy yards at Wilhelmshaven, was for a long time the Navy's 'lucky ship' until beaten by an opponent superior in technology and tactics. The battleships, 761 feet overall and with a 100-foot beam, could reach 31·5 knots with their 160,000 h.p. engines. Besides nine 11-inch guns in triple turrets, they carried twelve 5.9-inch guns in twin turrets and numerous light and heavy AA guns: fourteen 4.1-inch, sixteen 37 mm and up to 28 20 mm. In the illustration above, two Arado 196 aircraft are mounted on the *Scharnhorst*'s catapults, her total complement of aircraft being four. On operations the ships' crews numbered around 1,900.

The Z-Plan Adventure

'At least from one country in the world we have nothing to fear in the way of an arms race,' suggested the Earl of Beatty, Admiral of the Fleet in the Second World War, in the House of Lords on 26 June 1935. This 'one country' was Germany, and the Earl went on to add that the British should be truly grateful to the Germans for it. A week earlier, on 18 June, Britain's Foreign Minister Sir Samuel Hoare and the German Special Ambassador Joachim von Ribbentrop had signed the Anglo-German Naval Treaty in London. The German Reich had undertaken to limit the size of its naval forces to 35 per cent of the combined fleets of Britain and the Commonwealth. The 35 per cent applied also to each individual category, and therefore to battleships, cruisers, aircraft carriers, destroyers and so forth. One exception was submarines: in this case Germany was permitted to build the equivalent of 45 per cent of the British tonnage, and, furthermore, was to be allowed to file an application, at a given time, to bring her submarine force up to the strength of the British. The advantages for Germany were clear: till now she had secretly violated the arms limitation clauses of the Treaty of Versailles; now this conduct had been legalized. For the first time, an erstwhile enemy nation had, in a two-page treaty, given its assent to the creation of a German Navy, and had, with a stroke of the pen, shelved the Treaty of Versailles.

The 35-per cent clause, however, also gave a firm promise of safety for Britain in that there could be no recurrence of the naval rivalry and arms race between Britain and Germany that had taken place at the beginning of the century. It meant, too, that Berlin recognized London's maritime interests and accepted British supremacy at sea as an unchallengeable fact. As the German Navy could grow only to just over a third of the size of the Royal Navy, and also had to contend with its less favourable geographical position in relation to the open sea, it seemed absurd to consider England as a naval opponent once again. In the event, the German Navy took the Naval Treaty very seriously in the years immediately following. According to the then Chief of Naval Staff, Rear-Admiral Günther Guse, it was 'the basis for an enduring understanding with England'. Raeder went even further: he issued explicit instructions forbidding even a theoretical study or war game involving England as the enemy. Hitler had already affirmed in 1933 that he would never go to war against England, Italy and Japan, and he was constantly restating this assurance to his Commander-in-Chief of the Navy, Raeder, who believed Hitler's promise. 'It was the tragedy of my life', the Admiral of the Fleet later wrote, 'that events developed in a quite different direction'.

A more realistic assessment of the politics of the Third Reich and their consequences can be drawn from events in the Navy in the summer of 1938. Again it was Hitler who, at the end of May, in the heat of the first crisis between Berlin and Prague, summoned Raeder and told him that in the long run the chances were that England would be on the side of Germany's opponents. Hitler wanted the expansion of the Navy speeded up in preparation for a conflict which he thought would not commence until 1944, and in the meantime Raeder would be at liberty to build up his fleet.

This news, though widely forecast, nevertheless came as a surprise, and posed the Navy considerable problems. According to the classic sequence of every planning operation a concept had to be established of the way a naval war against Britain could successfully be waged before a decision could be taken as to the types of ships that should be built to meet the demands of this concept. Raeder commanded his youngest staff officer, the ever-critical Commander Hellmuth Heye, to plan and produce a document on waging a naval war against England. Additionally, he called for a planning committee on which the most experienced admirals were to mould 'a united plan for the build-up of the Navy in all its aspects'.

With clear-headed reasoning, Heye maintained that the decisive major sea battle, the meeting of armoured giants such as had once taken place at Jutland, offered Germany little prospect of turning the strategic situation at sea in her favour. He went on to point out that this would still be the case even in the unlikely event that Germany were able to send into action a fleet as large as or larger than the enemy's. If, as was to be expected, Germany could field only an inferior force, then the prospects for achieving her objective *with battleships* were nil.

This opinion shocked many, particularly the more elderly of the admirals. Did the naval command now intend to scrap the battleships? Was it no longer true that a navy would stand or fall by the number of its armoured giants?

Heye's alternative proposition was that the primary task was to wage war against Britain's maritime trade. He emphasized that a campaign of this type, bearing in mind Britain's dependence on overseas trade, promised the greatest possible success. In consequence, only ships ideal

Future opponents lie peacefully side by side. The German Navy sent its newest pocket battleship, *Admiral Graf Spee*, (foreground) across the Channel for George VI's Coronation Review in May 1937. The ship lies in Spithead Roads beside the British battleship *Revenge* and the battle-cruiser *Hood*, then the biggest warship in the world.

Admiral Scheer in the Bay of Biscay, photographed from the airship *Graf Zeppelin*. The crew has crowded forward to wave to the airship. At high speed, as in the picture, *Admiral Scheer* had a range of 9,100 miles; at lower speeds her range was wider. Because of their wide radius of action these first diesel-powered big ships could steam over the oceans without relying heavily on land bases.

for cruising warfare roles on the high seas should be built. However, there was a snag: these ships would have to pass through the North Sea to reach the Atlantic. They would therefore have to break through the British blockade. How would they do it? The advocates of the surface battle fleet came bounding back with their answer: only the biggest ships would be able to fight their way through into the open Atlantic.

So opinion swung back once again to the concept of a mighty battle fleet, in spite of recognition of the fact that it would be impossible to defeat Britain in the foreseeable future with battleships. Yet it seemed unthinkable that a navy could be planned which would bring the Reich naval supremacy, even world supremacy, and not include battleships.

The young Commander Heye could not make much headway with his counterplan against the massed might of the admirals. In fact he would hardly have made any headway at all, for he was sceptical even of the alternative to the battleship concept, namely the U-boat wolf-pack campaign against enemy shipping. At the time it was generally accepted that anti-submarine forces, equipped with improved position-finding methods and techniques, could force the attacking U-boat on to the defensive and thus enormously reduce its chances of success. The voices of the German submariners, who did not agree, were heard by the planning committee as little as were those of the representatives of the Luftwaffe, who must have thrown into the debate the consideration—a crucial one—that even the most heavily armoured battleships could no longer be relied upon to withstand attack from the air. On 31 October 1938 the chairman of the planning committee, Vice Admiral Guse, laid before the Commander-in-Chief, who had kept out of the discussions, the fruits of his committee's deliberations. Besides a more powerful *Panzerschiff* class for hunting down and destroying merchant shipping over large areas of sea, the committee recommended above all the building of six super-battleships of the *H*-class which were to have a displacement of more than 56,000 tons. The Navy evidently wanted to prove itself worthy of the prestige of the German Reich.

Raeder went immediately to Hitler and presented him with the details of the 'Z-Plan' for the expansion of the Navy. In doing so, he recalled later, he offered the following alternatives. On the one hand Germany could build principally U-boats and *Panzerschiffe*; this could be done quicker and, in the event of war, would represent a positive threat to Britain's sea-trade lifelines; however it would be a lop-sided process, as such a force would not be much use in a battle against heavier British naval forces.

On the other hand Germany could create a striking force in the form of a battle fleet made up of the most powerful battleships possible; this would take longer to achieve than the first alternative, but once complete such a fleet would be in a position to wage war against both merchant shipping and naval forces with real prospects of success.

The already-begun construction of the battleships *Gneisenau* and *Scharnhorst*, at 31,850 tons nearly three times the displacement permitted by the Versailles Treaty, was sanctioned by the Anglo-German Naval Treaty. Yet with their nine 11-inch guns they were at a disadvantage against enemy battleships. Both ships were to have been equipped later with 15-inch guns, but nothing came of this in the war.

'The Germans' most fervent wish was never to go to war with Britain again,' said Hitler on 1 April 1939 at the launching of the battleship *Tirpitz* at the Navy yards at Wilhelmshaven. At this time the Z-Plan adventure, with its ambitious aim of matching Britain's naval power, had already begun. On the same day Dr Erich Raeder, Commander-in-Chief of the Navy, was promoted to Grand Admiral. Before the month was up, Berlin had unilaterally repudiated the treaty with Britain.

Recommending the second solution, Raeder added a word of warning: the Navy would be unready if war were declared in the next few years. Hitler repeated his assurance that the fleet would not be needed before 1946. He, too, like the admirals, favoured building the big ships.

The starting point for the 'Z-Plan' came on 29 January 1939. Three months later Germany repudiated the naval treaty with Britain. The dream that Germany would never again take up arms against Britain was nearly over—and four months later war broke out.

The Z-Plan fleet, which in view of subsequent events proved to be a monumental miscalculation, envisaged by 1944 the six super-battleships already mentioned, powered by diesels and with a main armament of eight 16-inch guns. Additionally, there were to be: two battleships of the *Bismarck* class and two of the *Gneisenau* class, the latter to be re-armed in 1941–42 with 15-inch guns; three new battle-cruisers of 32,000 tons, armed with 15-inch guns and capable of particularly high speeds—a class which by 1948 was planned to number 12 ships; two 23,000-ton aircraft carriers, the first of which, the *Graf Zeppelin*, had been launched on 8 December 1938. Progress towards its completion continued intermittently, and finally halted in 1943; five 10,000-ton heavy cruisers, the so-called Washington cruisers; as well as four new light cruisers and nine patrol cruisers, 47 destroyers, 54 torpedo boats and a total of 229 U-boats of various types from the 'canoes' to the long-range U-cruisers.

The last-mentioned light naval forces, apart from the U-boats, were supposed to be substantially strengthened in numbers in the years up to 1948, giving a projected final total of 24 light cruisers, 36 scouting cruisers, 70 destroyers and 78 torpedo boats.

Yet it was not the small ships but the time-, manpower- and material-consuming battleships that justified doubts as to whether the capacity of the German shipbuilding industry would be able to cope with this mammoth programme. Apparently the OKM hoped to be able to tap the entire workforce of German industry and build new production plants without paying the least heed to the needs of Hitler's highly-prized army and Luftwaffe.

The early outbreak of war caught the Z-Plan in the first stages of its execution: only the keels of two *H*-class super-battleships had been laid, but these soon had to be dismantled. The battle for industrial capacity and priority now took hold. On 3 September 1939, as all the grandiose plans were dissolving about him, Admiral Raeder was still trying to justify the Z-Plan policy: 'In 1944–45 Germany should have enough battleships, *Panzerschiffe*, cruisers, aircraft carriers and U-boats to challenge Britain's supremacy at sea.' The question was whether Britain would stand idly by while all this activity went on.

The Sail Training Ships

On 26 July 1932 the Navy suffered a tragedy: the old sailing vessel converted into the sail training ship *Niobe* capsized off Fehmarn in a squall and took 76 men to the bottom with her. After this disaster the 1933-built *Gorch Fock* and her sister-ships *Horst Wessel* (1936) and *Albert Leo Schlageter* (1937) were built with safety as the primary considerations. They had better sea-keeping qualities than most cargo ships.

The *Gorch Fock* had a sail area of 1,800 square metres, while her slightly bigger sister-ships had a sail area of over 1,975 square metres. These white ships sailed on many training voyages in the far north, to the Atlantic islands, and as far as the West Indies. They rode out many a storm, and sailed for decades after the war under the American, Portuguese and Soviet flags.

In the summer of 1939 the political situation in Europe became more and more critical. The Navy did not seem very concerned about this, as Hitler had given assurances that there would be no war against England in the next few years. Thus the battleship *Gneisenau* (above) carried out Atlantic trials without a single round of live ammunition aboard, and normal training of U-boat and destroyer crews went ahead in the Baltic. It was only in the middle of August 1939 that the Navy began to make preparations for the outbreak of a war whose imminence, even at the last moment, it did not want to believe.

The First Offensive

The war began with the attack on those units of the Polish Navy that had not already left the Baltic. In the Gulf of Danzig, mostly naval aircraft and minesweepers operated. The picture shows a flotilla of *M35* class minesweepers (682 tons, 18 knots, two 4.1-inch guns) after completing a task.

The first major operation in the war at sea against Britain: minelayers, cruisers, destroyers and torpedo boats laid the 'West Wall' mine barrier to secure the German Bight against a thrust by the Royal Navy. Britain in her turn declared her blockade of Germany on 3 September 1939. In this picture mines ready for laying are seen on the deck of a torpedo boat.

The pleasure steamers *Roland* (foreground) and *Cobra* were converted into minelayers and used to fill out gaps in the minefields in the German Bight.

Minelayers, escorted by motor minesweepers, alter course preparatory to minelaying.

The first big success of the German U-boats was gained by Lieutenant Otto Schuhart, seen here (right) on the conning tower of his Type VIIA boat. On 17 September 1939 Schuhart hit the British aircraft carrier *Courageous* with two torpedoes, and the 22,500-ton carrier sank within fifteen minutes with the loss of 518 men.

In most respects the few German U-boats conducted the war on merchant shipping strictly according to the rules. They had to surface, stop the ship, and search it for contraband goods. This armed British steamer was sunk by a torpedo fired from the stern tube of the U-boat.

At the beginning of the War the U-boats' guns—the Type VII had a 3.5-inch—still served an important purpose. After surfacing it was necessary to be quicker into action than an armed opponent. According to international law a ship could not be sunk until its crew was safe.

Prien's *U 47* in Scapa Flow

The war was just six weeks old when Germany hailed her first hero: Lieutenant Günther Prien. Following careful planning by the U-boat operations staff, Prien, commanding *U47*, penetrated into Scapa Flow, the main base of the British fleet, on the night of 13/14 October 1939. He remained surfaced, the sky lit only by the flickering northern lights, passing through the treacherous currents of the Kirk Sound, which, as aerial photographs had shown, was not yet barred with blockships. The British Admiralty had proposed that it be blocked, but the government considered the cost too high. After several weeks of indecisive delay the blockship that was to do the job left London—on the same day as Prien entered Scapa Flow.

The U-boat commander and his crew were bitterly disappointed. The latest aerial reconnaissance before the sailing had established the presence in Scapa Flow of one aircraft carrier and five heavy ships. Now it looked almost empty, except for the silhouettes of one or two big warships just off the mainland. Two minutes before 1 a.m. the U-boat moved in for a surface attack. The quadruple torpedo tubes were fired by the officer of the watch, Lieutenant Engelbert Endrass, but one torpedo failed to leave the tube—and the other three missed. Prien turned the U-boat round and fired the stern torpedo: another miss. At this crucial moment the torpedoes had let them down.

In the middle of Scapa Flow, his mission not yet accomplished and his torpedo tubes empty, Prien gave the command to reload with the reserve

Battleship salutes U-boat: in the Kiel inlet the *Scharnhorst*'s crew lines up to welcome home the *U47* after its success in Scapa Flow. Lieutenant Prien is on the conning tower. On its tenth mission against the enemy, *U47* was sunk with all hands in the north Atlantic.

torpedoes. The order was carried out in record time, and after only a quarter of an hour two tubes were ready to fire again. Prien had no desire to wait any longer, for his boat might be spotted by patrol vessels at any moment. He personally conducted the second run-in and at 1.22 a.m. the old battleship *Royal Oak*, which was lying at anchor, was hit by two torpedoes and blew up. 833 British seamen died.

U47 steamed back out of Scapa Flow by the same route, unscathed, and entered Wilhelmshaven three days later. Prien was the second naval officer, after Grand Admiral Raeder, to receive the *Ritterkreuz*, and U-boat chief Karl Dönitz was promoted to Rear Admiral on the deck of *U47*. The German propaganda machine made the most of this success, though a discreet silence was of course maintained on the matter of the torpedo failures.

Yet this was not the first occasion on which a U-boat crew in an advantageous situation had gone into attack and after an unnerving wait had had to conclude that its torpedoes had failed. Several U-boats had themselves been sunk by enemy action after similar unsuccessful attacks. The torpedo failures, which reached a catastrophic level during the occupation of Norway, led to the first serious crisis of confidence in the German Navy. They were not to be eliminated until the summer of 1940.

Two U-boat aces, Günther Prien and Joachim Schepke (right), seen reconstructing a convoy battle with glasses. Both were killed in March 1941 when the British anti-submarine forces hit back for the first time.

Admiral Hermann Boehm (left) was the first Commander-in-Chief of the Fleet in the War, but after personal disagreements with Grand Admiral Raeder, he was replaced in October 1939 by Admiral Wilhelm Marschall (right). Even Marschall's operations, however, in spite of a good measure of success, did not meet with the undivided approval of the Naval Staff in Berlin.

The first sorties by both fleets yielded no results. Here is the battleship *Gneisenau*, escorted by a destroyer and an anti-submarine aircraft. The British Home Fleet also made several sorties into the North Sea, but the two sides never met.

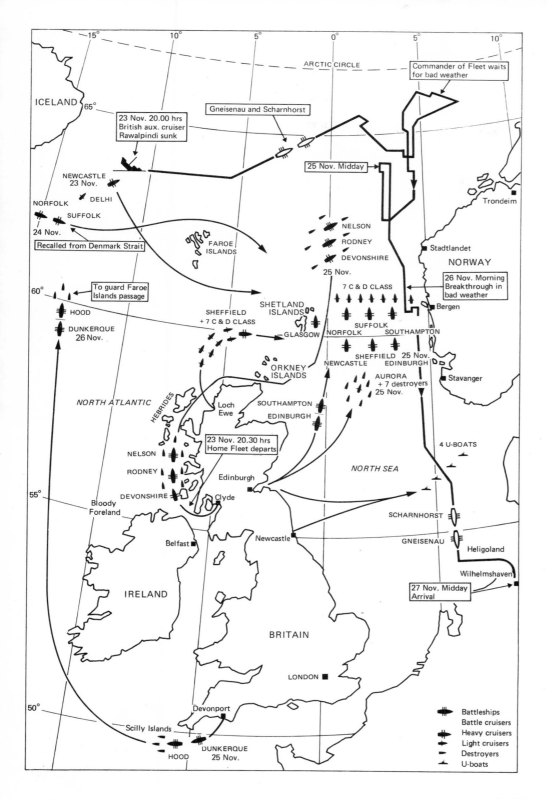

ARCTIC CIRCLE

ICELAND 65°

Commander of Fleet waits for bad weather

23 Nov. 20.00 hrs British aux. cruiser Rawalpindi sunk

Gneisenau and Scharnhorst

25 Nov. Midday

Trondeim

NEWCASTLE 23 Nov.

NORFOLK   DELHI

SUFFOLK

24 Nov.

Recalled from Denmark Strait

Stadtlandet

NELSON

RODNEY

DEVONSHIRE

25 Nov.

NORWAY

26 Nov. Morning Breakthrough in bad weather

FAROE ISLANDS

7 C & D CLASS

To guard Faroe Islands passage

60°

HOOD

DUNKERQUE 26 Nov.

SHEFFIELD + 7 C & D CLASS

SHETLAND ISLANDS

GLASGOW

Bergen

SUFFOLK

NORFOLK   SOUTHAMPTON

ORKNEY ISLANDS

NEWCASTLE

SHEFFIELD   25 Nov.
EDINBURGH

Stavanger

NORTH ATLANTIC

HEBRIDES

Loch Ewe

SOUTHAMPTON

EDINBURGH

AURORA + 7 destroyers 25 Nov.

4 U-BOATS

23 Nov. 20.30 hrs Home Fleet departs

NELSON

RODNEY

DEVONSHIRE

Edinburgh

Clyde

NORTH SEA

55°

Bloody Foreland

Belfast

Newcastle

SCHARNHORST

GNEISENAU

Heligoland

Wilhelmshaven

IRELAND

27 Nov. Midday Arrival

BRITAIN

LONDON

50°

Devonport

Scilly Islands

HOOD

DUNKERQUE 25 Nov.

Battleships
Battle cruisers
Heavy cruisers
Light cruisers
Destroyers
U-boats

In the 'November sortie' *Gneisenau* and *Scharnhorst* made a surprise appearance in the Faroe Islands passage and sank the British armed merchant cruiser *Rawalpindi*. The map shows how the entire British fleet hunted the German ships in vain.

51

The River Plate Drama

On 17 December 1939, shortly after 6 p.m., the German pocket battleship *Admiral Graf Spee* left the harbour of Montevideo on the River Plate, in which it had spent the last 72 hours effecting repairs to damage inflicted in battle. The ship's movements were being followed by thousands of people all over the world. Everyone expected that she would sail out to renew battle with the superior British force that was lying in wait for her on the open sea, but events took a quite different course. Before leaving the neutral three-mile limit, the crew of the *Graf Spee* transferred to a freighter, and the much-admired pocket battleship was scuttled, on the orders of the commander, Captain Hans Langsdorff.

This, Britain's first significant success in the war, was won by psycho-

The pocket battleship *Graf Spee*, pictured above in port at Hamburg, and on the right in the south Atlantic with a dummy turret (arrowed) meant to make the ship look like a British cruiser. After a successful commerce-raiding voyage, in which she sank nine British ships between 30 September and 7 December 1939, she encountered Commodore Harwood's squadron with the cruisers *Exeter*, *Ajax* and *Achilles* on 13 December. *Exeter* and *Ajax* were severely damaged in the engagement that followed, but *Graf Spee* was also hit, and ran into Montevideo for repairs.
52 This proved to be a fatal move.

logical means. British representatives in Montevideo had unleashed a war of nerves by creating the impression that a battle-cruiser and an aircraft carrier were waiting to intercept the German ship, while in fact they were still a long way off. Although the naval high command in Berlin had different information on the enemy's strength and position, Raeder left Langsdorff to make his own decision, and he elected, in view of the apparently hopeless situation, to destroy the ship and save his crew. For the German leaders, and particularly for Hitler himself, this was a crushing blow to their belief in the striking power, and even invincibility, of their big ships.

Graf Spee had used up more than half her ammunition in the fight. Another battle, with the big ships rumoured to be awaiting her, would have been beyond her. Her commander therefore gave the order to scuttle her, and took his own life on the same day—as if to show that he had not acted out of cowardice. On the left is a scene from Captain Langsdorff's funeral in Buenos Aires. The crew were interned in Argentina.

One of the German Navy's most successful operations was the secret mine offensive carried out by destroyers in the first winter of the War. They completed eleven minelaying missions just off the English coast—and even in the Thames estuary—undetected and without any loss. The Allies lost 67 ships and several destroyers on the mines.

The hard winter of 1939—40 hindered naval action in coastal waters. Estuaries on the Baltic and the North Sea froze over, and even icebreakers were often unable to keep a passage open. Training and weapon testing suffered particularly. New torpedoes could not be tested and the torpedo crisis was thus delayed until winter was over.

The torpedo boat *Iltis* in a heavy swell. In February 1940 forthcoming events had already begun to cast their shadows over the scene. The German fleet tanker *Altmark* had supplied the pocket battleship *Graf Spee* in the south Atlantic and had taken over the crews of British ships sunk by her. On her voyage home *Altmark* took shelter on 16 February 1940 in Jössing Fjord in Norway, where she was attacked by a boarding party from the British destroyer *Cossack*. The British released the 303 prisoners. Norwegian warships did nothing about it. The *Altmark* incident strengthened Berlin's impression that Norway was not prepared to protect her neutrality against British intrusions. A few days later Hitler ordered preparations for operation *Weserübung*, the German attack on Norway.

Operation *Weserübung*

'The *Altmark* incident clearly shows that Britain in the long term has no intention of respecting Norway's sovereign rights.' This was stated in the directive issued by the *Wehrmacht* high command for Operation *Weserübung* on 26 February 1940. Nor could the possibility be excluded that Britain would occupy certain key points on the Norwegian coast in order to prevent the Germans using neutral waters, or that Britain would establish air bases in Norway. 'In this case', the directive went on, 'action must be taken to forestall a British occupation of Norway by occupying it ourselves. As long as Norway remains neutral and holds fast to her neutrality, there are no grounds for occupation. But if this situation is threatened, Norway must be brought under our control . . .'

A brief review of British plans and aims will show that the German fears were not altogether without justification. Although, on 2 September 1939, Germany had declared the inviolability of Norway so long as this was not infringed by any other nation, Britain's First Lord of the Admiralty, Churchill, was, by 19 September, already occupied with the possibilities of cutting off the vital supply of Swedish ore to Germany *via* Narvik, as a memorandum shows. As the ore carriers had to pass through Norwegian waters on the most dangerous part of their journey, nobody had any valid right to interfere with them. Churchill's plan to mine the Norwegian coastal route had not been agreed by the British government in 1939.

When, at the end of November 1939, the winter war between Russia and Finland had broken out, the Western powers saw a further opportunity for intervention. They offered an expeditionary force of three to four divisions, which was to march through north Norway and Sweden to Finland and at the same time occupy Narvik and the Swedish ore mines. But the Scandinavian countries refused the offer of help, and Finland avoided an Allied intervention by calling a ceasefire with the Russians on 12 March 1940. On 28 March the Allied high command took up Churchill's suggestion and decided to mine the Norwegian waters on 5 April. Shortly afterwards they would occupy various Norwegian ports and harbours. In the event, German action anticipated the planned Allied moves only by a very short space of time.

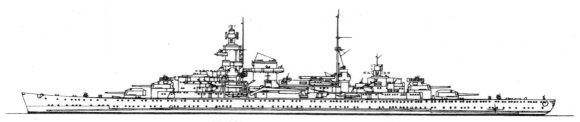

Admiral Hipper, one of the five heavy cruisers laid down in German shipyards after the 1935 naval treaty, though only three saw service under the German flag. At 14,000 tons they were considerably bigger than the so-called Washington cruisers, but only carried eight 8-inch guns. Their 132,000 h.p. turbines gave a maximum speed of 32·5 knots, but range was limited and it looked as if, for the German Navy's purposes, their construction was a mistake.

Mountain troops embark on the *Hipper* at Cuxhaven. The cruiser is to join the four destroyers of Warship Group 2 and enter Trondheim on the morning of 9 April 1940. The operation is entirely dependent upon secrecy, for the German fleet has to pass through the Bergen–Shetlands passage on the day before the occupation, and superior British forces could intercept it at this point.

Operation *Weserübung* began on the night of 7 April, when the fleet and various other warships sailed from Germany. Early in the morning of 9 April the capital, Oslo, and the ports of Kristiansand-Süd, Bergen, Trondheim and Narvik in the far north were to be simultaneously occupied. In contrast with the army and the Luftwaffe, which took part in the operation with comparatively small forces, the Navy had to put practically the entire German fleet into action. On the Navy alone depended the successful occupation of the ports. The commander of the Naval Group East, Admiral Rolf Carls, calculated that about half of the forces involved would be lost.

While the German fleet was steaming north on 7 and 8 April, in the teeth of an ever worsening storm and in heavy seas, the British too were on the way, to carry out the long-planned mining of the Norwegian coastal waters. Yet it was only by coincidence that an engagement took place. The British destroyer *Glowworm*, separated from the rest of the group by the bad weather, sighted some isolated German destroyers and eventually found herself in combat with the German cruiser *Hipper*. During this engagement the *Glowworm* rammed the *Hipper*, but ran under the cruiser's bow and was destroyed. The *Hipper*, though leaking badly, got under way again with the troops on board and set course for Trondheim as planned.

In a south-south-westerly gale the German task force heads northwards on 7 and 8 April, the 14 destroyers suffering particularly in the bad weather. The following sea lifts them and plunges their bows deep into the water, making it difficult for them to maintain course and maintain speed. The waves smash the equipment of the mountain troops on deck and sweep men overboard. Rescue attempts are useless, and the ships carry on battling their way northwards.

The sea boils against the side of a destroyer. Lifelines crisscross the deck, but when a wave hits a man he cannot hold on.

Events take a dramatic turn on the morning of 8 April 1940. In the widely scattered German force the destroyer *Bernd von Arnim* engages a British destroyer which is coping much better with the heavy seas. The C.-in-C. of the Fleet sends the cruiser *Hipper* to help. Suddenly the British ship, the *Glowworm*, belching black smoke, appears just off *Hipper*'s bows and turns to ram her. Her bows shattered, *Glowworm* finally capsizes close to *Hipper*. The Germans rescue 38 British survivors.

The Captain 'D', Commodore Friedrich Bonte, led ten boats to the attack on Narvik, and was killed on the morning after the occupation in the first British surprise attack.

The wrecks of the three destroyers *Arnim*, *Lüdemann* and *Zenker*, which were scuttled in Rombaksfjord when their ammunition was exhausted.

Opposite page: mountain troops land in Narvik from the destroyer *Hans Lüdemann.*

On 13 April 1940 a British force, including the battleship *Warspite* and nine destroyers, closes for the decisive attack on the German ships in and near Narvik.

Severely hit and abndoned by her crew, the destroyer *Erich Giese* drifts into the fjord outside Narvik before capsizing and sinking.

The northernmost goal, the ore port of Narvik, had ten destroyers under the command of Commodore Friedrich Bonte heading towards it. For the mountain troops on board, about 200 on each destroyer, it was undoubtedly the worst sea voyage of their lives. The storm had broken up the group, but in the early morning of 9 April it assembled again in the quieter waters of Ojotfjord. Orders were to 'try to make the operation look like a friendly operation', but off Narvik the German ships were confronted by the coastal warships *Eidsvold* and *Norge*, which opened fire and gave battle until they were blown to pieces by German torpedoes. At this point Narvik capitulated, and was occupied by General Dietl's mountain troops.

The destroyers now badly needed to refuel for the return voyage, as the British fleet had put to sea to engage the Germans as soon as news of the German action arrived, yet only one of the two tankers ordered to Narvik had turned up. Fuelling took a long time, and in the early morning of 10 April, in a ferocious blizzard, British destroyers made a sudden attack on the German destroyers lying at Narvik. The German destroyer leader *Wilhelm Heidkamp* with Commodore Bonte on board blew up after being hit by torpedoes; the *Anton Schmitt* sank, and two more were damaged. The other German ships gave battle and succeeded in sinking the British *Hardy* and *Hunter*.

Three days later another British force led by the battleship *Warspite* steamed into Ojotfjord. The German U-boats, lying in position, were unable to hold up the enemy's advance, as their torpedoes failed, and this time all the remaining eight German destroyers in Narvik were destroyed, or were scuttled after firing their last shells. The destroyer crews joined the mountain troops in Narvik, but this distant outpost was now completely cut off.

Severe losses were also incurred elsewhere. In Oslofjord the new heavy cruiser *Blücher* sank after artillery and torpedo fire from the Norwegian

'We build fine-weather ships, lovely to look at, but no use in the Atlantic.' This criticism came from a naval architect. Shown here is the *Blücher*, whose commissioning was delayed by her being altered five times. Without adequate trials and without having fired a single live round, *Blücher* was sent to capture Oslo—and was sunk by the Norwegians in the Dröbak narrows.

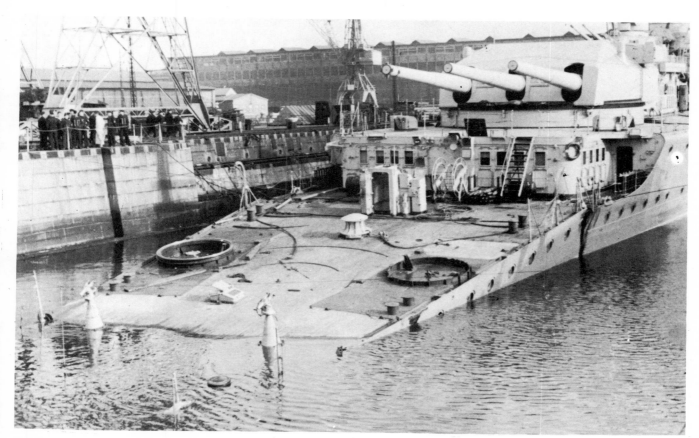

fortress of Oscarsborg in the Dröbak Narrows. Contrary to all the signs that he should not do so, the commander of the 5th warship group in Oslofjord, Rear Admiral Kummetz, had tried to get through the Dröbak Narrows without first securing the fortress with storm troops. The Norwegians did not lose the opportunity he thus offered, and opened fire, with devastating effects. On the return journey out of the Oslofjord the cruiser *Lützow*, formerly the pocket battleship *Deutschland*, was badly damaged by a torpedo from a British submarine. The *Lützow* limped back to Kiel, but was henceforth eliminated from the oceanic cruiser warfare for which she had been intended. The naval high command described the use of the ship in the Norwegian venture as a 'grave strategical error', but Hitler himself had given the order that sent it there.

Operation *Weserübung* brought the German Navy its first severe losses, as well as the bitter disappointment of the complete failure of the U-boat torpedoes. Yet Norway fell into German hands, the northern flank of Europe was secured from Britain's clutches, and Germany's range of operation bases was extended. Thus eventual success could be said to have justified the losses.

The *Lützow* in Kiel with her stern broken off, the result of a torpedo fired by the British submarine *Spearfish* on *Lützow*'s return voyage from Oslo. *Lützow* was out of action for a year. She had formerly been the pocket battleship *Deutschland*, and was renamed on Hitler's orders—for no ship bearing the name *Deutschland* could be allowed to sink.

Operation Juno: the German fleet made a surprise attack on the British withdrawing from Norway, sinking a troopship and destroying the carrier *Glorious*. The lower picture shows the battleships *Scharnhorst* and *Gneisenau* in action at full speed.

After the German U-boats' astonishing initial successes in the autumn of 1939 and the crisis over torpedo failures, which reached catastrophic proportions in the Norwegian venture (31 torpedo attacks from good firing positions against warships and transports brought not one success), the U-boat force, in the early summer of 1940, had to start all over again. For three months the battle against Britain's trade lifelines had been stilled. Now it was to be renewed under much more favourable conditions, for the rapid collapse of France gave the German Navy possession of France's Atlantic ports. Lorient, Brest, La Pallice and St Nazaire became U-boat bases, tailor-made for the Atlantic battle. For the U-boats this meant the end of time-wasting voyages through the North Sea and round the British Isles, and thus increased the amount of time they could spend at the patrol area. Their successes increased proportionately.

Thus there began in the summer of 1940 one of the longest, bitterest and most fluctuating battles of the Second World War, the battle of the Atlantic. It commenced with a short period in which individual U-boats were able to notch up high scores. Allied merchant shipping had lulled itself into complacency, the U-boat menace seemed to have disappeared, and convoy protection was very weak, the latter because the Royal Navy needed its destroyers and escorts for the evacuation from Dunkirk and other French ports and later for defence against the feared German invasion of England.

In this phase of the struggle the U-boats sought and found their enemy off the North Channel, where British merchant traffic abounded. Like wolves the U-boats fell singly upon the herds of ships and claimed one victim after another. In June 1940 Rear Admiral Dönitz sent out three

The Bid for the Atlantic

U29 under Lieutenant Schuhart sinking a Greek steamer laden with war material for England at the beginning of July 1940. The stern torpedo tube of the Type VIIA U-boat can clearly be seen out of the water.

Only one third of the available front-line U-boats was normally in the theatre of operations. Of the other two thirds some were on their way to or from operations and others were in their bases being overhauled or re-armed. Here, torpedoes are being taken on.

U-boat groups at short intervals, and for a while up to nineteen U-boats were operational in this theatre at any one time. Thus June became the most successful month so far in the war against enemy shipping: 63 ships totalling 355,431 gross registered tons fell to the U-boats alone, and altogether Allied shipping suffered losses of about 600,000 gross registered tons—far more than they could build at this time.

Success or failure in the battle for the Atlantic depended on a very simple formula: if the Germans were able to sink more ships than the Allies could build as replacements, Britain would inevitably weaken. Britain's new Prime Minister, Churchill, recognized the danger that could paralyse his country, and later wrote that what really worried him during the war was the U-boat threat.

Yet the U-boat force was still much too weak to exploit the opportunity to the full. After every successful attack on a convoy the U-boats had to return to base to re-arm, leaving the Atlantic clear of wolf-packs. Thus several convoys reached their destinations unscathed.

The U-boat Staff imagined how different the story would be if they had one hundred boats at the front . . . or even the three hundred that Dönitz had consistently advocated as necessary for England's defeat. Before the war the U-boat building programme had progressed at a snail's pace.

Running repairs had to be carried out on long operational voyages, both on the narrow deck and in the cramped interior of the U-boats.

According to the Z-Plan the building of battleships took priority, as Raeder and the naval high command expected great strategical gains from them, and the U-boat was given little chance for the future. On the outbreak of war a sharp turnabout was executed. Suddenly 29 U-boats per month were to be built, but it was years before this target was reached.

In the meantime the war took its own toll. 28 German U-boats were lost in the first twelve months, most of them in the North Sea and the North Atlantic, while in the same period only 28 new boats were completed. In reality, the U-boat force was weaker than it had been at the beginning of the war, for of these 28 new boats, 10 were of the small Type II, whose range was not sufficient for Atlantic operations. Some of the older Type II boats were withdrawn from the front and assigned for training duties. After all, what use would it be to build new boats if they could not be handed over to trained crews?

By February 1941 the number of U-boats available for operational service fell to its lowest level, 21. Twenty-one as against the 300 that Admiral Dönitz needed to paralyse Britain's maritime trade. A hand had indeed been reached out towards the Atlantic, but its grip was too weak. At the same time the British anti-submarine force was building up. The battle was moving into a new and tougher phase.

U-boats slice through the stormy Atlantic towards their ordered positions. The boats' main weapon are the four bow torpedo tubes in the crew's living quarters. The bunks are hooked up out of the way while the torpedoes are prepared for loading.

Hydroplane operators in the U-boat's control room. Their job was to keep the boat at the required depth no matter what was going on.

Repairs to the diesel engines had to be carried out in a very confined space.

The commander, already wearing sou'-wester and oilskins, takes one more look around through the periscope before giving the order to surface. Even in heavy seas the U-boats had to travel on the surface in order to gain the extra speed available from their diesels, which would enable them to outpace a convoy and thus take up a good attacking position.

The more boats that could be gathered
together to patrol a certain area, the
better the chances of encountering a
convoy. A round-the-clock watch would
then have to be kept for smoke on the
horizon. All too often such efforts went
72 unrewarded.

One of the U-boat force's most thorny problems was how to find enemy convoys or single enemy ships in the wide expanses of the Atlantic. This task would have been best undertaken by a combination of aircraft and U-boats, but the Navy had no aircraft of its own. The few available long-range reconnaissance aircraft were mostly employed by the Luftwaffe for other duties. Even when, for a while early in 1941, Admiral Dönitz succeeded in getting together a long-range group of 4-engined Focke Wulf aircraft for joint operations with his U-boats, the collaboration all had striven for was not always crowned with success. Later, when the battle of the Atlantic took the U-boats even further from Europe's coasts, the aircraft, which were land-based, simply did not have sufficient range.

Therefore it was mostly up to the U-boats themselves to track down their prey—apart from the information received from German naval radio intelligence concerning convoys which had sailed and their mean course. Unfortunately, however, the conning-tower of a U-boat on the surface was only about 15 feet above sea level, and because of this, U-boats had a severely restricted range of vision—so restricted, in fact, that a convoy could pass by only 20 miles away without being spotted by a U-boat because, for the U-boat, the convoy lay below the horizon.

Thus the sharpest possible look-out was a prerequisite for every success, and it was for this reason among others that Dönitz wanted more U-boats —in order to have more 'eyes', more boats combing an area and thus making it difficult for an enemy convoy to escape the broad U-boat sweeps. If a U-boat sighted a convoy, it passed the word along to the other boats in its group. The pack gathered and then, generally at night, made its attack.

U-boats: the Reconnaissance Problem

The higher above sea level the look-out's eyes, the wider the radius of his vision. Here the periscope is being used as an observation position. The extra six feet could mean an increase in range of up to three miles.

A member of the crew reports number 2 bow torpedo tube fired. Moments later the target tanker is hit, explodes and sinks. In autumn 1940 the U-boats began their battle against convoys, finding their defences unexpectedly weak. But the situation was soon to change.

A U-boat surfaces close by some ship-wrecked sailors. U-boats attacked at night and on the surface. The flames from a blazing tanker illuminate the battlefield.

A jubilant return to base, a 'birthday' for the crew. In the first year of the war 28 boats were lost, the same number as were built.

After the initial elation of a safe return, the hard work began again. The commander had to give U-boat chief Rear Admiral Dönitz a detailed report of his operations. Every event, every contact with the enemy and every torpedo fired was gone over. The pictures show Lieutenant Adalbert Schnee (right) and Lieutenant Hans Jenisch (below) giving their reports at U-boat headquarters.

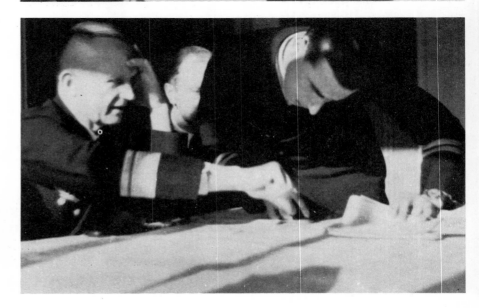

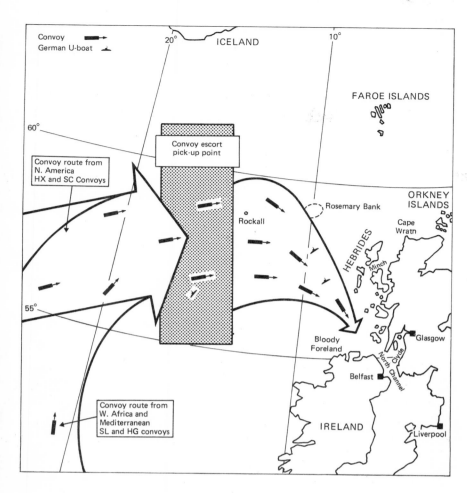

The map shows the approaches to the North Channel used by convoys bound for England. It was in this area that the U-boats operated in autumn 1940 and winter 1940–41, and that the first convoy battles were fought.

In March 1941 British anti-submarine forces struck back. Several boats with experienced commanders—among them Prien (below), Kretschmer (below, left, receiving the *Ritterkreuz* from Grand Admiral Raeder) and Schepke—were lost in the battle. Admiral Dönitz abandoned operations in the North Channel and sent his U-boats further out into the Atlantic.

Operation Sealion

One abortive episode was Operation Sealion, the invasion of England planned to take place after the occupation of France in the summer of 1940. Although the Navy had managed, with quite inadequate means, to put together an invasion fleet, Grand Admiral Raeder repeatedly warned Hitler of the risk involved in such a venture. A landing in England, he asserted, in the face of a nation committed to fight to the last, and whose naval supremacy was indisputable, could not be considered the 'extended river crossing' that the army liked to call it. Hitler agreed, and only with hesitation agreed to the mounting of the operation. A landing should only be considered if Germany won air supremacy over southern England, if a course for the fleet had been secured through the thick minefields on both sides, and if the British fleet could be tied down elsewhere and thus prevented from disrupting the invasion force. These were conditions unlikely to prevail; Hitler was therefore glad to have an opportunity to let the matter drop. In fact he was preoccupied for a long time with the attack against Russia, hoping that a rapid victory in the East would shatter Britain's last hope of winning the war.

Small landing craft in rough water on the Channel coast. The Army considered the planned landing in England as a mere extended river crossing. The Navy warned that this would not be so.

A sceptical eye observes the barges assembled at the Rhine port of Duisburg–Ruhrort and converted for use as landing craft. They were to have been towed across the Channel by tugs.

Soon loading exercises was going on all along the German-occupied Channel coast. Motor vehicles and armoured scout cars could be loaded by the bow ramps—but how were they to be disembarked under fire on hostile shores?

Other barges in the invasion fleet were to be powered across the Channel by airscrews. The waiting British destroyer flotillas would have shot them to pieces along with the rest of this infinitely vulnerable armada.

Ocean Raiders

'The Naval high command is convinced that the course the war is taking justifies plans for the re-birth of the battleship.' This sentence appears in a memorandum issued by Raeder's closest aides in July 1940. As the war seemed as good as won, the high command was already planning the build-up of the fleet in the ensuing peace. Not U-boats but battleships were the 'principal weapons in the oceanic battle against the enemy's supply lines'.

But as the war was not yet actually won, the battleships and other heavy ships would soon be able to prove whether the high command's theory was correct. The circumstances seemed particularly favourable: Europe's coastline, from the North Cape to the Pyrenees, was in German hands—a strategic situation undreamed of a few months before. What was true of the U-boats applied also to the battleships—they needed only to break through the British blockade of the northern sea routes. Once in the Atlantic, they could withdraw to the French Atlantic bases at any time they wished. The battle against the enemy's merchant shipping, using surface forces, was about to begin, and the high command in Berlin were pinning all their hopes on it.

The first ship on the scene was the heavy cruiser *Admiral Scheer*, one of the two former pocket battleships still available, which suddenly turned up in the West Atlantic in November 1940. *Scheer* attacked a poorly protected convoy, sank a number of ships and wrought havoc on the Allied convoy system. After this success she set course southwards, to appear equally suddenly in another area, where she struck and again vanished. This hit-and-run system proved a headache even for an enemy superior in numbers, for his ships could not be everywhere at the same time to meet the attacks.

One month after the *Admiral Scheer*, the heavy cruiser *Admiral Hipper* also got through the stormy Denmark Strait into the North Atlantic. The ship rode out many a fierce storm, suffered mechanical breakdowns, and sighted not one convoy—till Christmas Day, when it located and attacked a strongly protected troopship convoy. Opposition was so fierce, however, that *Hipper* was forced to break off the attack and ran—for the first time—to put into the base at Brest.

At the beginning of February *Hipper* steamed into the North Atlantic again and, near the Azores, came upon a convoy from Sierra Leone. At the same time the commander of the fleet, Admiral Günther Lütjens, took advantage of a spell of bad weather to break through into the North Atlantic with the battleships *Gneisenau* and *Scharnhorst*. His orders were

Admiral Scheer took no part in operations in the first year of the war owing to the long time she spent in dock. The picture shows her after she had been remodelled as a heavy cruiser. She was to be the most successful of the German pocket battleships.

to make trouble, and, more specifically, to destroy all shipping heading towards Britain.

Thus, with four heavy ships in the theatre, the time had clearly come for the surface ships versus U-boat controversy to be resolved. The aim was to sink as many ships as possible, and therefore to prove that the battleship was truly the principal weapon in the ocean battle against the enemy's supply lines. Now the battle was on, and the British too brought in their battleships, to shield the priceless convoys. The German ships had orders not to engage an equal opponent, so Admiral Lütjens was unable to report any immediate successes in his log. He spread his net into the middle of the Atlantic and over the coast of West Africa. In the middle of March the two battleships attacked a large number of ships sailing alone as a result of their convoy breaking up, and sank thirteen. With this success under their belts the fleet commander headed his ships back to Brest, and a few days later the cruisers *Hipper* and *Scheer* returned safely to Germany.

It looked like a great victory, and the picture was made even rosier by the fact that two new ships, their trials and training completed, were waiting in the Baltic for their first assignment: the 41,700-ton battleship *Bismarck* and the latest heavy cruiser *Prinz Eugen.* If they got through the Denmark Strait into the North Atlantic and there joined forces with the *Gneisenau* and *Scharnhorst*, out of Brest, the fleet commander would have

The gun on the deck of this English merchant ship offered only symbolic protection against the sudden attacks of German raiders in the South Atlantic. *Admiral Scheer* took on the work of her sister ship *Graf Spee* a year after the latter's spectacular end. She caused a great deal of trouble among Allied shipping.

The heavy-cruiser type was unsuitable for long-range ocean operations because of its limited range and unreliable engines, though *Admiral Hipper*, shown here, was used precisely for this purpose.

Admiral Hipper noses out of Brest behind a mine-clearance vessel for a brief Atlantic sortie. While on such operations the German ships were dependent on a system of supply ships for fuel and stores.

at his disposal in the open Atlantic a task force which need fear no enemy.

The British did not fail to appreciate the importance of this menacing development, and they took the fastest possible action: for the R.A.F., Brest was a target within easy range, and bombers were sent out to attack the ships in their berths. The first attack, by a force of 100 bombers, on the night of 30 March 1941, failed, but at dawn on 6 April the *Gneisenau* was badly damaged by a torpedo from a low-flying aircraft. Five nights later, four more bombs struck the ship.

Thus a few air attacks on the heavily defended port of Brest sufficed to disrupt the plans of the naval high command. The *Scharnhorst* had not in fact been hit, but engine repairs kept her stuck in dock for several months. What use were the unique strategic opportunities offered by the Atlantic bases on the French coast if their vulnerability to British bomber attacks could not be eliminated?

Admiral Günther Lütjens, in command of the fleet from June 1940, faithfully followed Raeder's instructions regarding the use of the big ships. Lütjens had no desire to be the third, after Admirals Boehm and Marschall, to quit the job through disagreements with the Naval Staff. His success seems to have proved him right. The picture on the left shows his flagship *Gneisenau* during Operation Berlin in February 1941, in a long Atlantic swell.

No one yet knew that the climax of the war on Allied merchant shipping, as waged by heavy surface forces, had already passed. As for its success, *Gneisenau* and *Scharnhorst*, *Scheer* and *Hipper* had, in the months gone by, between them sunk or captured almost 270,000 gross registered tons. This was a figure now achieved regularly, every month, by the handful of U-boats attacking Allied merchant shipping. It thus appeared that the battleship was not to play the dominant role in the struggle to disrupt enemy supply routes. Yet there was to be a further, more dramatic series of events before recognition of this fact dawned.

A watch on board the *Scharnhorst* in the north Atlantic. On the morning of 8 February 1941 a convoy is sighted east of Newfoundland, but in accordance with orders it is not attacked, as the old British battleship *Ramillies* is guarding it. Battle with an equal opponent is forbidden the German ships.

After long search sweeps the fleet moves to the central Atlantic and warmer latitudes. For those of the crew, off watch, an open-air concert is organized on deck.

A rare encounter in the Second World War. Off the coast of West Africa U-boat *U124* meets up with the battleships. There follows a combined convoy operation in which *Gneisenau* and *Scharnhorst* have to stay in the background as, once again, a British battleship is covering the convoy. But *U124* and *U105* move in and sink several ships.

The fleet flagship *Gneisenau* (above) and her sister-ship *Scharnhorst* (left) in the north Atlantic. The operation had been conceived by the high command as a test of the effectiveness of the big ships. Many similar operations were still to follow, but in reality the pinnacle had already been passed. Soon the fleet had to leave the Atlantic to the U-boats again.

The *Scharnhorst* in dock in her new base at Brest. After service in the Atlantic a machinery overhaul was unavoidable, and this pinned the ship down for several months.

The Royal Air Force made good use of the opportunity: on the right is an aerial photograph of the German battleships lying in dock. The bottom picture shows the first four-engined bombers attacking the ships. Because of constant repairs the ships could not be used again in 1941.

The docking of the battleships *Gneisenau* and *Scharnhorst* in Brest, and the return of the heavy cruisers *Admiral Scheer* and *Hipper* to Kiel spelt the end of the first, successful phase of the ocean raiding war. Now Grand Admiral Raeder and the naval high command pressed for further operations of this type to be undertaken, with a view to keeping up the pressure on the enemy's supply lines. In spite of the setback of having the two battleships in Brest out of action, plans for the next Atlantic operation, with the code-name *Rheinübung*, had already been planned. Fleet commander Günther Lütjens, armed with the super-battleship *Bismarck* and the heavy cruiser *Prinz Eugen*, was to repeat the success of his earlier operations in the Atlantic.

Outwardly the two ships looked much the same—their silhouettes, especially from far off, could easily be mistaken for one another—but in other respects, namely in size, firepower, range and ability to withstand attack, they were quite different ships. Thus together they did not form a homogenous force such as the two sister-ships *Gneisenau* and *Scharnhorst*. Admiral Lütjens would have preferred to wait until the second ship of the

The First —and Last— Voyage of the *Bismarck*

On 1 April 1941, after the heavy cruiser *Admiral Scheer* had returned safely home from a long, raiding operation in the South Atlantic, the crew was personally welcomed by C.-in-C. Raeder. Nobody yet suspected that the period of commerce raiding with heavy surface craft had just ended.

The climax and consummation of German shipbuilding: the 41,700 ton *Bismarck*, with its eight 15-inch guns the embodiment of concentrated force and power. Two ships of this type and six more of the even mightier *H*-class were to symbolize Germany's sea power. 89

The heavy cruiser *Prinz Eugen* was a fast and beautiful ship, yet her class was little suited for long Atlantic operations far from base. Only a system of supply ships made such voyages possible.

Bismarck type, the new *Tirpitz*, had completed her operational training. With these two, the most powerful battleships in the world, under his command in the Atlantic, prospects for a successful prosecution of the anti-merchant shipping campaign would indeed be rosy.

However, the Commander-in-Chief, Grand Admiral Raeder, was not prepared to wait any longer. The pause in the battle of the Atlantic had given the enemy a chance to consolidate his strength. As the year 1941 advanced, the nights grew shorter, and with them diminished the chances of stealing unnoticed into the Atlantic as they had done in January. Nor could the possibility be excluded that America might enter the war and completely alter the situation. Because of these considerations, Raeder decided that Operation *Rheinübung* should be set in motion immediately if it were not to be in danger of being called off because of increased and therefore unacceptable risks. On 18 May 1941 *Bismarck* and *Prinz Eugen* left the Baltic base of Gotenhafen. Two days later they passed through the narrow Kattegat—and were for the first time spotted by British agents. On 21 May British reconnaissance aircraft brought home photographs of the two ships lying in Korsfjord near Bergen and taking on more fuel oil. On

22 May they had vanished from the Korsfjord.

The British Admiralty immediately ordered all available forces to prevent the German battle group breaking out into the Atlantic. Reconnaissance patrols in the Iceland–Faroes passage and the Denmark Strait—the Germans' preferred northern passage between Iceland and Greenland—were increased. A battle-cruiser squadron and the Home Fleet itself steamed out in order to pin down the German ships wherever they tried to make their breakthrough. On the evening of 23 May the British cruisers *Suffolk* and *Norfolk* sighted the enemy, as expected, in the Denmark Strait, just off the pack ice. Their radio transmissions were picked up aboard the *Bismarck*, and Admiral Lütjens therefore knew that he was being shadowed. When the *Norfolk* emerged for a few moments from the mist and blizzards, into full view, the *Bismarck* attacked her with her main armament, but the British ships vanished, maintaining contact with their new radar apparatus. Lütjens knew that any attempt at concealment was useless, and the prospect of an unnoticed breakthrough, illusory. His course and position were known to the Royal Navy, and the enemy could now bring up his own big ships to do battle.

Similar in silhouette, yet radically different in size, fighting power, range and endurance: the heavy cruiser *Prinz Eugen* (top drawing) and the battleship *Bismarck* formed the German task force on operation *Rheinübung*. Both ships had been commissioned in August 1940, and at the beginning of 1941, tried, tested and with trained crews, were awaiting their first assignment. *Prinz Eugen*, built at Kiel, was, at 14,420 tons, the largest heavy cruiser in the Navy. Her turbines delivered 132,000 h.p., endowing her with a top speed of 34 knots, but her range was only 6,800 nautical miles at cruising speed. She had a crew of 1,600 men and was armed with eight 8-inch guns, twelve 4.1-inch and twelve 37 mm AA guns, up to 28 20 mm AA guns and twelve torpedo tubes.

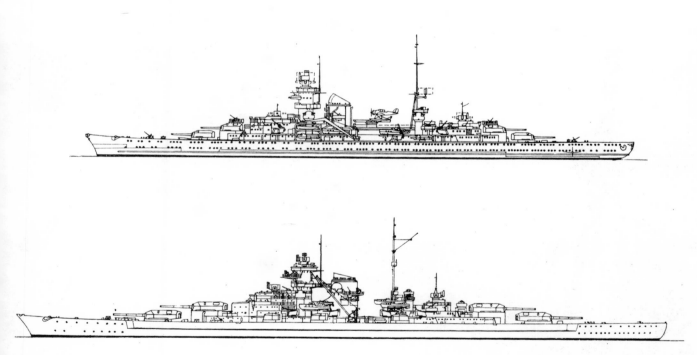

The *Bismarck*, built by Blohm & Voss in Hamburg, displaced 41,700 tons, was 823 feet long and had a beam of 118 feet. Her full complement on her first and last voyage was 2,092. Her 150,000 h.p. engines and triple screws gave her a top speed of 30 knots, and her armament consisted of eight 15-inch and twelve 5.9-inch quick-firing guns, sixteen 4.1-inch AA guns and sixteen 37 mm, as well as a number of light AA guns. She carried four aircraft which could be launched from a double catapult.

The after 8-inch turrets of *Prinz Eugen* firing a salvo. In the fight against the British battle-cruiser squadron, *Prinz Eugen* landed the first hits on the mighty *Hood*, herself remaining un-damaged.

The next stage in this story came in the early morning of 24 May 1941, in the brief but dramatic engagement between Vice Admiral Holland's battle-cruiser squadron, with *Hood* and *Prince of Wales*, and the *Bismarck* group. The British closed with the German ships, keeping them just off the bow and thus were only able to bring their forward guns to bear when they opened fire at 05.53 hours. At the outset there was even some un-certainty as to which of the German ships was the *Bismarck*, and con-sequently the attackers scattered their fire instead of concentrating on the foe's most important ship.

Two minutes later, at 05.55, Admiral Lütjens gave the order to open fire. The range was only 9 miles, and *Prinz Eugen* landed the first hits on *Hood*. Then came the fatal salvo from the *Bismarck*, which resulted in a direct hit on the British flagship's magazine. The *Hood* blew up. Only eight minutes after the engagement had begun this mighty ship had slipped beneath the waves. Now the Germans turned their guns on the second British battleship, and at 06.02, the first shots struck the *Prince of Wales*. The ship was brand new, its artillery and gunnery untried in action, and only individual barrels were firing. One minute later shell splinters mowed down practically all her officers. Numbed by this tragic turn that events had taken, and himself wounded, Captain Leach gave the order to turn

Cleaning the gun-barrels of 'Dora' turret on *Prinz Eugen*, and (below) taking on shells.

The C.-in-C. of the Fleet, Admiral Günther Lütjens, inspects *Prinz Eugen*'s crew before Operation *Rheinübung*. Behind him are the cruiser's Commanding Officer, Captain Helmuth Brinkmann, and the Executive Officer, Commander Otto Stooss.

An armoured colossus, held by many to be unsinkable: the *Bismarck*. Above the bow may be seen the 15-inch 'B' turret, the control tower, the admiral's bridge and the foretop gunnery control position.

away. All he could do was to try to evade the German's accurate and telling shellfire by withdrawing at full speed.

What happened next was, for the British, almost a miracle. The Germans did not take up the pursuit. It was within their power to destroy the damaged second ship as they had done the first, but they contented themselves with half a victory. The commander of the fleet, Admiral Lütjens, had his orders: his principal task was to sink merchant ships; he might only engage warships if absolutely necessary or if no great risk were involved.

Up till now German surface ships had always managed to enter the Atlantic unnoticed, this factor being an essential condition of successful surprise raiding, but the *Bismarck* group was being watched. Because of

the engagement in the Denmark Strait her position was known to all, and the British cruisers were maintaining constant contact, yet in spite of this completely altered situation, so different from what had been anticipated, Admiral Lütjens felt obliged to stick to his orders, however out-of-date, while no signal came from Berlin to grant him freedom of action in the light of events.

Meanwhile, the Royal Navy was bent upon hunting the *Bismarck* down, and avenging the loss of the *Hood*. The pursuit was to last for three days until, at a time when it already looked hopeless, it was crowned with success. These three days and nights were crammed with mistakes, wrong orders and accidents on both sides. At first the *Bismarck* parted company with *Prinz Eugen*; the heavy cruiser was not to be bound to the flagship

Bismarck, leaving harbour for Operation *Rheinübung* in line ahead, behind a mine clearance vessel. This photograph was taken from *Prinz Eugen*, following in the battleship's wake.

Topping up with fuel in the Korsfjord, near Bergen, before the breakout into the Atlantic. It was here that *Bismarck* was picked up by British aerial reconnaissance — and a day later her departure was also noted.

and its fate. *Bismarck* was losing oil from a hit in the forward part of the ship, which meant that she would be unable to operate for as long as a week in the Atlantic, and would instead have to try to reach a base before the week was up. Yet she felt herself unable to shake off the British watchdog cruisers, and so Lütjens saw no danger in sending home lengthy reports on the fight with the *Hood.*

Ironically, the weary British had in fact lost contact at this moment . . . and it was these signals from the *Bismarck* that enabled them to pick her up once more and establish her position. Unfortunately for the British, however, because of faulty entries in the plot in the flagship of the Home Fleet, *King George V*, they steamed after the *Bismarck* in the wrong direction.

For two nights and two days there was no sign of the *Bismarck*. Then she was spotted by a British flying-boat, already far south and on course for Biscay. The Home Fleet steamed south without much hope. Only the task force sailing from Gibraltar with the aircraft-carrier *Ark Royal* could now intercept the *Bismarck*, and in fact torpedo-planes from the carrier, after first mistakenly but unsuccessfully attacking one of their own cruisers, the *Sheffield*, dealt a fatal blow to the *Bismarck* in its steering gear, rendering the ship out of control and therefore a sitting target for its pursuers. The *Bismarck* sank after a fierce fight at about 10.40 hours on 27 May 1941, taking with it about 2,000 men, including the entire fleet staff. Only 115 survivors were picked up by the British.

Along the edge of the icefield, in mist, snow showers and sometimes dense fog, the German battle group steamed through the Denmark Strait between Iceland and Greenland. To help the following cruiser keep station *Bismarck* switched on a searchlight on her stern.

The heavy cruiser *Prinz Eugen* entered Brest on 1 June, but with the sinking of the *Bismarck* the brief period of oceanic surface raiding came to a close. No matter how hard Grand Admiral Raeder pressed, Hitler never again assigned his battleships to operations involving such a degree of risk.

From the evening of 23 May *Prinz Eugen* steamed ahead of *Bismarck*, on the C.-in-C. Fleet's orders. This caused confusion among the British next morning. On *Hood* they mistook *Prinz Eugen* for *Bismarck* and initially concentrated their fire on the cruiser.

After the Denmark Strait engagement *Bismarck* took the lead again. Her bows, hit by a shot from *Prince of Wales*, are noticeably lower in the water, and she is losing oil. Admiral Lütjens decided to head for Brest.

This, one of the most famous photographs of the Second World War, shows *Bismarck* firing a broadside during her fight with *Hood*. Just six minutes after fire was opened *Hood* received a direct hit in the magazine and blew up. The victor survived only three more days, before being located and sunk by the British fleet.

The Channel Breakthrough

The shock that the unexpected loss of the *Bismarck* gave the German leadership upset the relationship between Hitler and the Commander-in-Chief of the Navy. 'Though till then he had in general given me a free hand', Raeder recalled, 'he now became much more critical and increasingly insisted on the correctness of his own views.' A few months later, when the question arose of what should be done with the big ships, the two men for the first time found themselves in violent disagreement.

In the meantime, the situation in Brest, forever in danger from air attacks, had become progressively more intolerable. Not only was there the *Gneisenau*'s severe torpedo damage to repair; the *Prinz Eugen*, which had come through the entire *Bismarck* saga unscathed, was hit by a heavy bomb on the night of 2 July 1941. This penetrated into the gunnery control centre and killed fifty men, the ship itself being put out of service until the end of the year. As for the *Scharnhorst*, her engine repairs had only

The battleship *Scharnhorst* under heavy camouflage. The constant threat of bombing raids on the French Atlantic ports forced the Navy to hide its valuable ships under camouflage netting.

Prinz Eugen too looks more like a ghost ship under camouflage. Bomb damage and repairs kept the fleet, which had been sent to Brest in expectation of great things, stuck in port. Raeder wanted to operate them in the Atlantic, but Hitler would not allow it.

just been completed, when she too was knocked out of action, by five bombs which hit her at La Pallice.

Only one year previously the naval high command had boasted of the unique strategic opportunities afforded by the bases on the Atlantic coast of France, and had pinned great hopes on them. Now, in spite of all efforts, it was proving impossible to protect the base against the ever stronger enemy air attacks, till it became apparent that the bases necessary for the ships' Atlantic operations no longer existed.

Grand Admiral Raeder and his staff refused to acknowledge this. Indeed, in the middle of November 1941 the Navy chief reported to Hitler's headquarters that the ships would be ready to resume operations in the Atlantic theatre in February 1942. Hitler, though deeply preoccupied with the war in Russia, did not agree. To Raeder's amazement he demanded to know whether it would be possible to bring the ships home through the Channel. 'Out of the question', declared Raeder and the naval high command. Yet

12 February 1942, Operation Cerberus. The fleet steams through the English Channel in line ahead, escorted by destroyers and torpedo boats. This operation was ordered by Hitler against the will and the warnings of the Naval Staff.

Hitler returned to this concept several times in the following weeks. He considered Europe's north flank threatened. If, as he feared, the British established themselves in Norway, it could be of enormous significance to the outcome of the war, and in order to prevent such an invasion he would need the German fleet, particularly the big ships. Therefore they must be brought back from Brest. 'The best thing to do', cried Hitler, 'is to steam up the Channel completely unexpected!' And if the Navy could not accept such a scheme, then the ships would have to be withdrawn from service in order that at least their guns and crews could be saved.

In spite of being offered this appalling alternative, Grand Admiral Raeder stuck to his conflicting view: 'The return of the Brest forces through the Channel', he told Hitler on 8 January 1942, 'will in all probability result in total losses or at least severe damage.' Nevertheless, the order for the Channel breakthrough was given. It was to be one of the best prepared and best coordinated operations carried out by German forces in the Second World War.

Although the British were completely in the picture regarding the German ships' state of readiness, and were on the alert for a dash through the Channel and the Straits of Dover, the Germans, by dint of a brilliant tactical move (and a lot of good luck), were able to take them by surprise. This tactical move was as follows: contrary to what was generally expected, namely that the breakthrough group would try to cover the most dangerous part of the journey under cover of night, the German schedule was planned so that the ships would pass within sight of the coast of England at midday and in broad daylight. It seemed more important to leave Brest in darkness, for their departure would not be noticed and reported, and the enemy could not prepare a reception for them. The element of surprise would be all the more effective, and would confuse the British, if the ships appeared off the English coast at a time when not a soul was expecting them.

Luck too lent a helping hand, for the radar reconnaissance network operated by British aircraft, an ingenious system devised especially for

Hour after hour, the fleet steamed up the Channel, and the British made no move. They had certainly reckoned on the Germans trying a breakthrough, but not at this particular time. The escorting aircraft were ordered to fly low in order to deceive British radar, but the numerous aircraft blips were the first sign that something unusual was going on in the Channel.

The heavy cruiser *Prinz Eugen* cleared for action. The heavy AA guns have just driven off a British bomber attack. The quadruple 20 mm AA guns on the forecastle and on 'B' turret wait for low-fliers to break through the outer flak barrier. This cruiser alone fired over 5,000 rounds of AA ammunition during the run through the Channel.

the night hours, broke down on the crucial night. But one question remained unanswered: how long could the undoubtedly numerous enemy intelligence agents in Brest be kept in the dark about the ships' departure?

On the evening of 11 February 1942 Brest was on an air raid alert. As usual, the harbour was shrouded in a smoke screen to confuse airborne attackers. At about 23.00 hours, while the alert was still in force, the ships slipped out of their berths, under cover of the smoke screen, and steamed out of the harbour undetected. The leading ship was the *Scharnhorst*, carrying the commander of the group, Vice Admiral Otto Ciliax, followed by the *Gneisenau*, with the *Prinz Eugen* astern. They were escorted by six destroyers, which in the course of the voyage were to be joined by numerous torpedo boats, minesweepers and E-boats. The force passed the Channel Islands and Cherbourg during the night without being spotted. When dawn broke it was in the Seine Bay and steaming at top speed north-eastwards. From this point on three German fighter squadrons provided constant air cover.

Nine o'clock, ten o'clock and eleven o'clock came and went without a hint of trouble. It was uncanny. Only from ten o'clock onwards German nuisance raids on the English radar stations gave a hint to the enemy that some unusual operation was taking place in the Channel. Then aircraft kept on being picked up on the radar screens, aircraft that apparently were circling over ships, the latter moving a high speed . . . In England, nobody

The view from the admiral's bridge of *Prinz Eugen*, ploughing through the wake of the ship ahead. The fleet is steaming at 28 knots through the danger zone, and on the bridge a watchful tension reigns. The heavy artillery opened up when British destroyers tried to close for a torpedo attack.

A dramatic moment in the Channel breakthrough: *Scharnhorst* has hit a mine off the Schelde estuary and lies motionless. The other ships steam past the flagship, which for a quarter of an hour has insufficient power even for her guns, but the enemy does not attack. After twenty minutes of hard work the boilers get up steam again, and half an hour after the explosion *Scharnhorst* is steaming after the fleet at top speed.

quite knew what to make of all these manifestations, and it was shortly before midday before the pilots of two Spitfires on reconnaissance saw the ships with their own eyes and reported them. Even then, a further hour and a half had gone by before the British stirred from their apparent paralysis.

First, shots were fired by the guns at Dover, but the ships were already at the limit of the guns' range. Next, six torpedo planes attacked—they were all shot down. Then came motor torpedo boats, bombers and destroyers, but all were unable to break through the protective ring. Finally, at 15.28 hours, something happened that threatened the success of the whole mission. Off the mouth of the Scheldt the flagship *Scharnhorst* hit a magnetic mine and lay stopped. The flotilla swept by, and the Admiral transferred to a destroyer, but half an hour after the explosion the damage was repaired, and the *Scharnhorst* got under way and raced after the other ships. In the North Sea both battleships struck mines but they did not stop them.

The Channel breakthrough ended as a great tactical success. Yet nobody realized that, in vacating the French bases, the fleet had already begun its strategic retreat.

Scharnhorst has made it! Happy faces line the rails as she enters Wilhelmshaven. The success of this operation caused great gloom in Britain.

The Channel breakthrough would not have succeeded if minesweepers had not tirelessly cleared the big ships' path before them. The picture shows a flotilla of motor minesweepers steaming to carry out this task.

The Heavy
Cruiser
Prinz Eugen

Prinz Eugen, the 'lucky' ship that survived the Atlantic operation and the Channel breakthrough without damage, was sent to Norway a few days later with *Admiral Scheer*. British reconnaissance spotted the ships and they were several times attacked from the air, without success. But on 23 February 1942 the British submarine *Trident* scored a torpedo hit on *Prinz Eugen* off Trondheim. The cruiser's stern broke off, but she was able to reach Trondheim under her own power. There the stern was made watertight and a jury rudder rigged (picture above), but she had to return home for repairs. As *Gneisenau* in Kiel had in the meantime suffered severe bomb damage, all three ships that had taken part in the daring Channel dash were now out of action.

The Mediterranean Theatre

In September 1940 Admiral Raeder realized the decisive significance of the Mediterranean in the fight against Britain. He saw the winning of the Mediterranean as the alternative to Hitler's assault on Russia. The Italians were too weak to maintain dominance over the Royal Navy in the Mediterranean. The British, operating from Alexandria and Gibraltar, with aircraft carriers (right) and other craft, were supporting Malta, which lay like an awkward obstacle on the path from Italy to North Africa. In autumn 1941 the situation in the Mediterranean was so serious for the Axis powers that German U-boats were sent in *via* the Straits of Gibraltar to commence operations in this new area.

The German U-boats had a good deal
of success in the Mediterranean. *U81*,
under Lieutenant-Commander Guggen-
berger, sank the British carrier *Ark Royal*
(above) off Gibraltar, and *U331*, under
Lieutenant von Tiesenhausen, sank the
battleship *Barham* off North Africa. The
carrier *Eagle* (below) was sunk in August
1942 by torpedoes from *U73*, under
Lieutenant-Commander Rosenbaum.

This British type *H*-class destroyer sailed under the German flag in the Mediterranean. *Hermes*, built in Glasgow in 1939 for the Greek Navy, was taken over by Commander Rolf Johannesson in Salamis in March 1942. She carried out convoy-escort and anti-submarine duties in the Aegean and protected North Africa-bound transports.

Britain's Lifelines Threatened

U46, commanded by Lieutenant-Commander Endrass, got home safely in spite of being rammed by one of her victims. In the middle of 1941 Admiral Dönitz extended the area of operations from the coast of Greenland to the Straits of Gibraltar and West Africa. The battle against Britain's vital supply lines was now being waged by the U-boats alone, including Italian ones (left).

One of the most successful U-boat commanders, Lieutenant Herbert Schultze, congratulating his crew on their decorations. Schultze put to sea in his new Type VIIA U-boat, *U48*, in April 1939 and commanded it with only one break until the end of June 1941, when it was withdrawn from operational service (below). During this period *U48* sank one escort vessel and 51 Allied ships, a total of 310,000 gross registered tons—by far the biggest figure achieved by a single U-boat in the Second World War.

After reaching rock bottom in February 1941, when Dönitz only had 21 front-line U-boats at his disposal, the number of operational U-boats began to increase rapidly as the intensive U-boat-building programme took effect. New crews were trained in the Baltic (the picture on the left shows the members of a commanding officers' training course) and the new boats spent five months in trials and training before being assigned to one of the front-line flotillas.

A U-boat sets out on operational patrol, led by a mine clearance vessel through the heavily mined coastal waters. The boats maintained radio contact with their headquarters on land and had to report regularly. If they did not report for several days and could not be contacted, they were presumed lost. Some got back despite appalling damage: *U333* (right) survived three rammings.

Drumbeat off America

After America's entry into the war in December 1941 a whole new theatre of operations was opened up for the U-boats. Shipping off the U.S. coast carried on almost as if it were peacetime, with no convoy system and little in the way of protection. Thus the few big Type IX U-boats that could be sent had an extraordinary success: between January and July 1942 460 ships, totalling 2·3 million gross registered tons, including many tankers (see below), were sunk in the area.

It took the U-boats about three weeks to reach the operation areas off the North American coast and in the Caribbean. Most of them were either on the way there or on the way back, having insufficient range and endurance to stay there long. The U-tankers—the Type XIV 'milch cows'—changed all this. They could carry 432 tons of fuel to replenish front-line U-boats and extend their operational period by several weeks. Torpedoes, too, could be supplied to U-boats in the pre-arranged areas. The lower picture shows a U-tanker riding high in the water as it returns empty to base after fuelling U-boats. As shown in the other pictures, supplying a U-boat was only possible in areas which no enemy aircraft were able to patrol. This 'air gap' closed when new long-range aircraft were pressed into service, and from 1943 on no part of the North Atlantic was safe for U-boats.

Meetings at sea became rarer from year to year. In general the boats of a U-boat group operating together never saw each other, their only contact being by radio-signal. As for bathing in the sea, in 1942 this could only be risked in out-of-the-way areas, as here in the South Atlantic.

Surprised from the air and attacked:
such nasty experiences were on the increase from early 1942, especially in
the Bay of Biscay. Flying either through
the cloud layer, or by night, British aircraft could appear over a target before
it had time to dive. Soon it became
clear that the enemy was using a
special type of radar, and from now on
the high frequency wave equipment
became an increasingly important
factor in the war at sea.

Air raids had driven the German battleships and cruisers out of their Atlantic bases. Not so the U-boats: concrete pens were built for them which could resist any bomb. The picture on the right shows Lieutenant-Commander Erich Topp's *U552* moving into its pen, while the bottom picture shows a returning U-boat being welcomed home. Till 1944, in spite of the severest bombing raids, not one U-boat was lost in the Atlantic ports.

An unusual view of the tear-drop shape of the U-boat, with its slim bow and forward hydroplanes. Even repairs necessitating dry docking could be carried out in the bombproof pens in the Atlantic ports.

The Battleship *Tirpitz*

The *Tirpitz*, built at the Navy yard at Wilhelmshaven, was very similar to her sister-ship *Bismarck* in construction and appearance, but, at 42,900 tons, she had a bigger displacement. She could also carry more fuel and thus had a range about 900 nautical miles greater than *Bismarck*. The picture of her in dock (right) gives an impression of the size of her propellers and rudder.

The largest German battleship, the 49,000-ton *Tirpitz*, never used its striking power against an enemy at sea. Success such as its sister ship *Bismarck* had found before being sunk never came its way. In 1941 the commander of the fleet, Günther Lütjens, had decided to delay the *Bismarck* operation until the *Tirpitz* was ready to sail too. The two ships together would have had a striking power that no rival could match. Yet Grand Admiral Raeder insisted that Operation Rheinübung should go ahead in May 1941, and at that time the *Tirpitz*'s crew had only two brief months of operational training behind them. *Tirpitz*'s commander, Captain Karl Topp, however, maintained that his ship was ready for action and suggested to the commander of the fleet that he should strengthen his battle group by the addition of the *Tirpitz*. Nothing came of this, for the naval high command wanted to send its second super-battleship into the Atlantic later in the year.

When the *Bismarck* was sunk, Hitler forbade his navy chief from any future Atlantic operations with big ships. Instead of continuing the Atlantic trade battle, *Tirpitz* and the heavy cruiser *Admiral Scheer* were to be transferred at the beginning of 1942 to Trondheim in Norway in order to guard against a British invasion of Europe's northern flank, which Hitler was afraid might take place. This was the beginning of the German presence in northern Norway, the 'fleet in being' which, through its

The 15-inch turrets 'C' and 'D' fire a practice salvo in the Baltic. *Tirpitz*'s heavy guns were never matched against an equal opponent at sea.

presence alone, constituted a strategic threat to the important supply route through the Arctic to Russia. The British were forced to surround their so-called PQ convoys in the Arctic with heavy naval forces in order to protect them from a possible attack by the German battle group.

In the event, *Tirpitz*, with Vice Admiral Otto Ciliax on board, left Trondheim on 6 March 1942 in order to attack convoy PQ12, which had been spotted by long-distance reconnaissance. But she did not go undetected. The British submarine *Seawolf*, stationed off the coast, reported *Tirpitz*'s movements. For the British an opportunity now presented itself to set a nearby battle group on to the *Tirpitz* and prepare for her the same fate as that of the *Bismarck*. The Home Fleet called up three battleships and an aircraft carrier for this purpose, but this activity did not escape the notice of the German radio intelligence. As ordered, *Tirpitz* turned around and was headed for home when, on 9 March, she was attacked by torpedo aircraft from the carrier *Victorious*.

In a furious battle lasting only eight minutes the *Tirpitz* escaped all the torpedoes and shot several of her attackers down in flames. Unscathed, she steamed back into the fjord, but even Raeder admitted that the ship's escape was a stroke of good luck. The fierce and resolute British attack

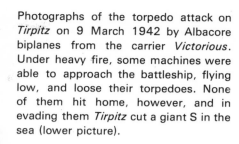

Photographs of the torpedo attack on *Tirpitz* on 9 March 1942 by Albacore biplanes from the carrier *Victorious*. Under heavy fire, some machines were able to approach the battleship, flying low, and loose their torpedoes. None of them hit home, however, and in evading them *Tirpitz* cut a giant S in the sea (lower picture).

made such a strong impression on the German leadership that they ruled that their ships were in future to leave their anchorage only when there was no danger of a British aircraft carrier becoming involved.

It was this fear of risks that led at the beginning of July 1942 to the hesitant start and later cancellation of the sortie by *Tirpitz*, *Scheer*, *Hipper*, *Lützow* and numerous destroyers, under the new commander of the fleet, Otto Schniewind, against the British convoy PQ17. Certainly the convoy, ordered to scatter by a panic Admiralty instruction, was almost annihilated by U-boats and aircraft. Yet the fleet came back empty-handed once again. Dissatisfaction grew among officers and men, and doubts were raised about whether this laid-up fleet might not have to forfeit its right to exist.

In early 1942 the heavy cruisers *Lützow* (right) and *Hipper* (below) joined the German task force in the north of Norway. *Lützow* was the unlucky member of the fleet. After being torpedoed with severe damage in April 1940, she had hardly been repaired before being torpedoed again in June 1941. While putting out against convoy PQ17 *Lützow* ran on to rocks on 2 July 1942 and was once again put out of action.

The 'fleet in being' made a strategic impression on the Allies merely by its presence in Norway. Yet the German force—the picture shows *Tirpitz*, *Hipper* and *Scheer* in a fjord—seldom went into action. Hitler's fear of the risks involved and the desperate shortage of fuel kept it locked up in its hiding place.

The Frozen Arctic

When Hitler overran the Soviet Union and sent his German armies deep into Russia, Stalin asked his Western allies for help. Supplies began to pour in across the seas, and as the ships came across the European Arctic and the Barents Sea to Murmansk, the German Navy and the Luftwaffe did everything in their power to disrupt the stream of war materials into Russia, which had to pass close to their own bases inside the Arctic Circle. This was to prove one of the toughest battlegrounds of the war, not only in terms of the fighting involved, but also in terms of the constant struggle against the weather.

The experiences of the German destroyers in the Arctic, among others, bear witness to this. On 28 March 1942 the 8th destroyer flotilla under Captain Gottfried Pönitz was ordered out against convoy PQ13, headed for Russia. Three ships, *Z24*, *Z25* and *Z26*, carried out a search for the convoy under a leaden sky and in poor visibility. Apart from a straggler they found nothing, but on the next day, in a dense blizzard, they suddenly fell upon the British escort vessels. In a blind struggle, some of it fought at very close quarters, *Z26* was shot to pieces by the British cruiser *Trinidad*. A picture of the burning and sinking German destroyer, of whose crew 96 were saved, shows the grim realities of the war at sea. But the *Trinidad* was also badly hit—by one of her own torpedoes which had run full circle—and she reached the Soviet harbour of Murmansk only with difficulty.

Two destroyers lying alongside each other in Altafjord, the anchorage of the German force in Europe's northern-most territory. In the foreground is *Z26*, behind her, *Friedrich Eckoldt*. Both sank in 1942 after dramatic fighting with British cruisers in the Barents Sea.

A few weeks later, the German Arctic destroyer group was ordered to attack convoy PQ14, then in Arctic waters. But they could find nothing. In fact the convoy had got stuck in the pack ice near Jan Mayen Island, and two thirds of the ships had turned for home because of the damage. Even if the destroyers had attacked the remaining one third, they would not have achieved much. The thermometer registered 15 degrees below zero, a Force 9 north-westerly gale was blowing, and snow and ice blizzards lashed the ships. They were coated in a thick layer of ice, the spray freezing on the superstructure. Binoculars and instruments were iced up, and the forward guns and torpedo tubes were frozen solid. The decks were mirror-smooth and it was impossible to stand upright on them, while the heavy seas forbade any attempt at de-icing. The Arctic in these conditions was hell for all those who had not only to sail in it but also to fight in it. The Senior Officer of the German flotilla, Captain Alfred Schulze-Hinrichs, gave up his hopeless assignment and turned for home.

Another two weeks later, on 1 and 2 May 1942, the destroyers were again on duty in the Barents Sea. A German U-boat had torpedoed the cruiser *Edinburgh*, but it looked as if the *Edinburgh* would still be able to make Murmansk. The destroyers tracked the *Edinburgh* down and gave her the *coup de grâce*, but lost their lead ship *Hermann Schoemann*, which received two hits in the engine room.

At about the same time, on convoy PQ15, the Allied escorts sank one of

The 5.9-inch gun on *Z25*'s foredeck completely frozen up, and the deck itself mirror-smooth with ice. The superstructure is coated in a thick shell of ice. Under conditions like these any action was out of the question.

Fog in the fjords and over the destroyers' berths (opposite); and an artillery duel in a stormy sea (below), the spray forming ice on the ship faster than it could be removed. It was under such conditions that the battle against the Russia-bound Arctic convoys had to be fought.

their own submarines, and the battleship *King George V* rammed a destroyer which avenged itself while going down, for its depth charges tore a large hole in the battleship's bottom. On 14 May the damaged cruiser *Trinidad* was sunk on her way home by an attacking Ju-88 dive bomber. These were the circumstances of the war in the Arctic, and so it continued for month after month and day after day.

For Germany, the high point of this bitter struggle was the scattering and subsequent destruction of convoy PQ17, out of which 36 freighters loaded with war materials for Russia were sunk. And for the British, the high point was the lucky escape of convoy JW-51B, on New Year's Eve 1942, in the middle of the Polar winter, from a German task force with the heavy cruisers *Hipper* and *Lützow* and six destroyers, which attacked in apparently favourable conditions but failed to hit home.

This failure had far-reaching consequences. Convinced by it of the uselessness of the big ships, Hitler ordered that the fleet be paid off and broken up. Grand Admiral Raeder protested bitterly, but in vain, and proffered his resignation. England, the German Navy believed, had won the easiest victory in its history.

Early morning on 2 May 1942 in the Barents Sea. While attacking the damaged British cruiser *Edinburgh* the German destroyer *Hermann Schoemann* received two hits in the engine room and lay stopped. In the midst of the fighting *Z24* came alongside the stricken ship and took off the crew, while *Z25* tried to conceal this manoeuvre by laying a smoke screen.

Hermann Schoemann abandoned. Scuttling charges had been set and in a few moments the ship sank. The British cruiser also sank, hit by another torpedo from *Z25*.

In the uncertain half-light of New Year's Eve 1942 the destroyer *Friedrich Eckoldt* steamed close to a ship she took for *Hipper*. In fact it was the British cruiser *Sheffield*, which sank *Eckoldt* with all hands under a hail of fire.

The long Norwegian coatline and the coastal route used for supplying the German ships were protected by numerous German flotillas. On the right are minesweepers operating in the fjords, and below are R-boat minesweepers. For all concerned, the polar winter was hard to bear.

These big 1,200-ton gunboats used off Norway by the Germans were armed with four 5-inch guns in twin mountings, and fell into German hands when the Dutch shipyards were taken over.

A U-boat's gun iced up in Arctic waters. In the face of opposition from Admiral Dönitz, Hitler insisted on stationing a strong U-boat group in Norway to guard against invasion. From 1942 these boats were allowed to attack convoys, but did not have the same success rate as in the Atlantic.

The Battle of the Atlantic

The longer the war against Britain lasted, the clearer it became that the Atlantic was the deciding factor, and that if the U-boat force could achieve real successes in the war against merchant shipping, the tables would be turned in Germany's favour. In the second half of 1941 the number of U-boats had significantly increased for the first time. In November 220 boats were in service, though 79 were on trials and 55 assigned solely for training duties. Of the remaining boats there were on 10 November 1941, 57 at sea in all, but only 22 actually in the operation area in the North Atlantic—that is, in the area which had to be decisive. The other boats were either outward- or inward-bound, in harbour for refit or new weapons—or, on orders from the supreme command, had to be transferred to other theatres: to the Mediterranean or the Arctic.

Day after day and week after week U-boats would plough through the stormy North Atlantic, on the surface unless forced by the enemy to dive, and always searching for convoys; for the side which could gain control of the Atlantic held the key to victory.

Admiral Dönitz, Flag Officer U-boats, made strenuous but vain efforts to stop his forces being split up in this way. He was convinced that the way to win the 'tonnage' war, the only one that could yield a decisive result, was to sink as many enemy ships as possible, and, from the economic point of view, to sink them where they were most vulnerable. The naval high command agreed that the concentration of U-boat effort should be in the Atlantic, but they had only temporary success with Hitler. When the catastrophe of having to supply North Africa from Italy became increasingly obvious in the autumn of 1941, he demanded the concentration of the main force of the Navy in the Mediterranean, and by this he mainly meant the U-boats.

The 'tonnage' war was a race between sinkings and launchings, and consequently the U-boat command sent their boats to the areas where they could achieve the highest daily rate of sinking. In 1941 these included the central and South Atlantic. The picture shows Lieutenant Jost Metzler on board *U69* returning to base after lengthy operations off the West African coast in the Gulf of Guinea.

One third of the front-line U-boats with experienced commanders now had to operate in the Mediterranean and the Arctic, and they left a huge gap in the Atlantic force. The figures for tonnage sunk or destroyed sank to an all-time low. The U-boat force had not paid sufficient attention to the imminent entry of America into the war to be able to complete in peace preparations for the surprise blow that they had intended to strike off the coast of America (see page 119). Thus began 1942, which was to bring the great turn in favour of the U-boats, together with heavy new responsibilities, for the force was still to be split up. The commander of the U-boats was not to be allowed to use his forces in the way he deemed right—namely in a concentrated effort to sink Allied tonnage. Yet in 1942

Whether under the tropical sun or in the raging storms of the North Atlantic, the key to the U-boats' success was their own ability to find targets. German radio intelligence picked up Allied signals and partly deciphered them, relaying important information on convoy movements, but it was up to the U-boats actually to find the ships, and they had no location apparatus on board to help them. In terms of technology, reconnaissance by U-boats had made little progress since the First World War.

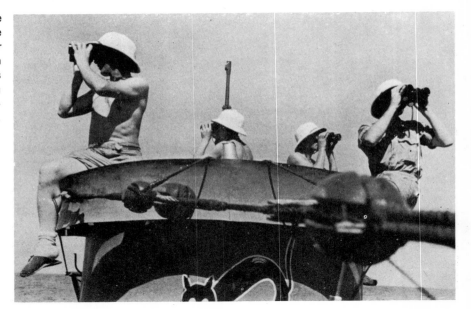

the battle for the Atlantic was moving ever faster towards its climax. At first no more than five U-boats could be mustered to operate off the coast of America, and at the end whole U-boat packs were fighting it out bitterly with equally strong Allied escort forces.

Up to the middle of the year, by which time they had organized their sea defences and above all had made their coastal sea routes safer from U-boats by the use of air patrols, the Americans had lost off their shores and in the Caribbean 460 ships totalling 2·3 million gross registered tons, including many tankers. From mid-July, Admiral Dönitz withdrew his U-boats from the coastal waters and re-assigned them to the North Atlantic convoy routes. This marked the beginning of a phase of wide-ranging attacks on merchant shipping, in which packs of 15 to 20 U-boats would comb an area of sea until one of them came across a convoy and summoned the others by radio.

The Allies met this concentrated attack on their lifelines by stepping up their defensive measures and concentrating on the U-boats' approach routes. As the experience of the escort groups grew, so did their tactics and equipment improve, while the convoys were now patrolled not just by their escorting vessels, but by aircraft patrolling large areas all around them. The long-range aircraft operating from Newfoundland, Iceland and Northern Ireland could, by 1942, fly 700 miles out into the Atlantic before having to turn back, which meant that the 'gap' in mid-Atlantic where convoys could not be provided with air cover became even smaller. Soon the U-boats recognized, in the aircraft which spotted them, attacked them, forced them to dive and thus drove them off, their most dangerous opponents.

But the U-boat packs were becoming more numerous too. There were 212 front-line boats at the turn of 1942–43, and if things had gone Dönitz's way, they would all have been focused on the struggle in the Atlantic. The battle became a race between the success of the U-boats in sinking ships and the capacity of British and American shipyards. Everything depended on whether losses could be met by replacements—or even outpaced by them. When 1942 closed, with another big convoy battle in the North Atlantic, the Allies by German calculations had lost 11·6 million gross registered tons in the past year and been able to build new ships totalling about 7 million tons. The race seemed to be going in Germany's favour—only they had overestimated their victories by about a third. In fact Allied losses in 1942 totalled 7·8 million tons, this figure being nearly

Garlanded with oak leaves, *U201* returns home in triumph in July 1942. Her commander Lieutenant-Commander Adalbert Schnee, was awarded the *Ritterkreuz*. Six months later *U201*, then under Lieutenant Rosenberg, was destroyed in a convoy action east of Newfoundland. With nine operational patrols and 25 ships sunk to her credit, she was one of the 30 most successful German U-boats. In 1943, on the other hand, many boats were lost on their first or second voyages.

The Flag Officer of the U-boats, Admiral Karl Dönitz, maintained a firm hold on the leadership of his forces. His command station, initially at Kernevel near Lorient, was moved to Paris from March 1942. With the chief of the operations section, Captain Godt (far right) and Lieutenant-Commander Schnee, a convoy-action veteran, Dönitz himself gave the boats their instructions by wireless. Often the convoys changed course and evaded the U-boats searching for them, rendering it necessary for U-boat command to anticipate the enemy's next move.

matched by the 7·2 million tons they built, while mass production techniques in the American yards were beginning to make themselves felt. In 1943 more than 12 million tons were built. Could the U-boats keep pace? The battle hung on the finest balance, and by early 1943 the outcome was destined to become clear.

Admiral Dönitz had forecast that three or four times the number of U-boats would be necessary to gain equal success against the ever more strongly protected convoys, and in February 1943 the turning point was reached. The important and valuable convoy SC118, with 61 fully laden ships, steamed into the middle of a U-boat formation. Yet *U187*, the boat that first sighted the ships and reported their position, was attacked and sunk by destroyers shortly after transmitting its message. Other boats found themselves tracked down too, and the extraordinary thing was that they were always pinpointed with great precision just after radio transmission. The convoy escorts possessed a marvellous new technical aid, an automatic radio direction finder which could show them the way to a signalling U-boat within seconds. The U-boats had no idea that it was

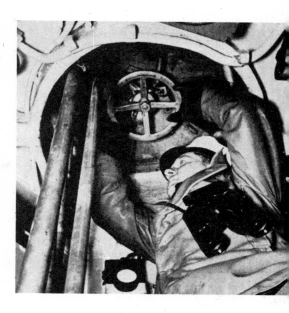

Alarm! A U-boat shadowing a convoy has been spotted by an enemy aircraft. The captain gives the order to dive and closes the conning-tower hatch behind him. The tanks are vented of air and the U-boat dives.

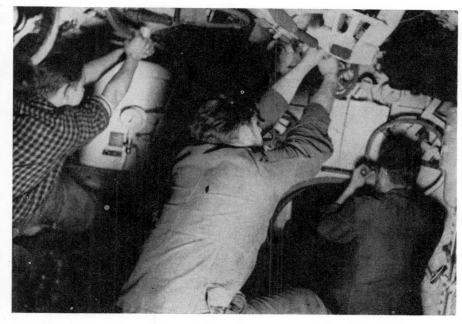

their signals that were leading the enemy to them, but anyway they *had* to report their sighting by radio, for only thus could U-boat control receive and signal to U-boats in the area the position of the convoys.

This, then, was what happened on convoy SC118. No fewer than 21 U-boats came on to the scene, but in the 4-day battle that ensued only five boats were able to fire torpedoes. All the others were quickly spotted, hunted and driven off. The convoy lost 13 of its 61 ships, but three U-boats were destroyed and four more severely damaged. In March 1943 the climax of the battle was reached. Fifty U-boats were lying in readiness in the Atlantic. Two big convoys, SC122 and HX229, came into their sights. As so often happened, the U-boats reaped their richest harvest on the first night's attack—14 ships were torpedoed and sunk. Then the convoy's defences were strengthened, and again and again the attackers were driven off, especially when they had just transmitted radio signals.

Only a handful penetrated to the heart of the convoy. The struggle continued for four days and nights before Dönitz withdrew his boats, their crews exhausted and the boats themselves unable, because of the enemy's strong air defence, to get near the ships. The U-boats thought they had sunk 32 ships, but in fact the figure was 21, totalling 141,000 gross registered tons, against which only one U-boat had been lost. This was the biggest convoy battle of the war. For the Allies, it was a major crisis: if they continued to suffer losses at this rate, the fight to keep supplies coming in would be lost.

It was at this decisive moment that the Allies were able to put in hand measures that substantially increased the convoy protection system. To the twelve escort groups that accompanied the convoys they added six roving support groups that could dash to the aid of convoys under attack. They also added three escort carriers, so that there was now scarcely a single spot in the Atlantic where a convoy was without air cover.

For the U-boats, convoys were now a very dangerous target. They were unable to repeat their success of March 1943. Above all, they suffered in May their own worst losses: 41 U-boats. Admiral Dönitz called the remaining boats back from the North Atlantic. He spoke of a postponement of the fight until better weapons were available, but the Allies' technical advances could no longer be bettered, and the convoys won through.

Once a U-boat had been located and forced to dive, a depth-charge bombardment would begin. All that those aboard the U-boat could do was keep calm and use their experience to try to escape. If the enemy broke off the attack, it usually meant that the convoy had left the area. The U-boat would surface and set after it.

Aircraft were the U-boats' worst enemy. 288 U-boats were lost at sea through air attacks. Aircraft could pick up U-boats on their radar as soon as they surfaced, and it was therefore difficult to get close to a convoy protected from the air.

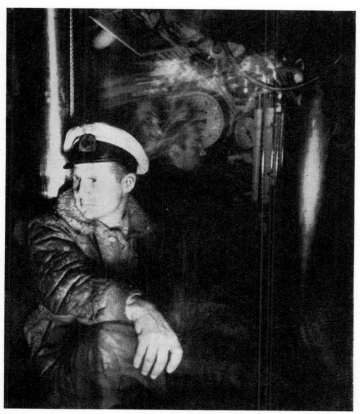

A U-boat commander sits in his control room listening for sounds that will announce the enemy's next attack. The boat's fate could hang on his making the right decision.

In 1943 some U-boats lured their aerial opponents into flak traps. These boats made no attempt to dive when threatened from the air, but met their attackers with a hail of fire. The picture shows *U441*, armed with a 37 mm AA gun and eight four-barrelled 20 mm AA guns. In spite of this armament she was sunk in the Channel by aircraft.

U-boats in
Distant Waters

From early 1943 onwards Type IX D2 U-boats—at 1,616 tons nearly twice as big as the Type VIIC Atlantic U-boats— were used on long-range operations. They had some success off South Africa and in the Indian Ocean, being based on Indonesia, then under Japanese control. They also operated in the Mediterranean, the picture on the right showing a U-boat leaving her base at Salamis.

German 'Monsoon' U-boats at the Japanese base at Penang (top picture). U-boats rendezvous with the tanker *Charlotte Schliemann* in the Indian Ocean.

Lieutenant-Commander Wolfgang Lüth received the insignia of the *Ritterkreuz* with Brilliants on his return with *U181* in October 1943 from the Indian Ocean. On 14 trips he had sunk 43 enemy ships. The picture on the right shows *U178* entering Bordeaux at the end of his voyage from Madagascar. The picture below shows fuel being taken on at sea.

The 'Channel Workers'

The Navy could not have carried on a war of aggression at sea without the Channel workforce, flotillas of little boats that escorted convoys, guarded the ports, cleared minefields and did battle with British fighter-bombers. The picture shows a minesweeping flotilla made up of former trawlers.

Patrol boats had to carry out their duties in all weathers. Here an armed trawler is seen off the coast of Holland.

Some minesweepers were effectively warships, even though after the M40-class they had to revert to coal-firing due to the oil shortage. They displaced 543 tons, were armed with two 4-inch guns and AA guns, and were also used to good effect for escorting German transports in the coastal shipping lanes.

Two 'Channel workers' pass on opposite
courses. Both have been camouflaged
against aerial reconnaissance.

Two small motor minesweepers leading
a convoy: these craft suffered heavy
losses at the hands of low-flying British
aircraft.

Old fishing vessels were pressed into service to hunt British submarines. Their only equipment for this specialized task was a hydrophone and depth charges. The picture shows a depth charge thrower being made ready on just such a 'submarine chaser'.

Transports carrying supplies to Norway were well protected. The picture shows the 18,160-ton former Norddeutsche Lloyd fast Far East steamer *Gneisenau*. In 1942—43 she was to be converted to an auxiliary carrier for 12 dive bombers and 12 fighters, but on 2 May 1943 she hit a mine in the Baltic and sank.

Coastal patrols had to deal with the recovery and defusing of lethal floating mines.

Motor Torpedo Boats in the Straits of Dover

The German motor torpedo boats (E-boats) were one type of 'Channel worker'. They transferred their bases after the occupation of France in 1940 to Dunkirk and Boulogne in order to attack British coastal traffic in the Straits of Dover. They were of between 80 and 100 tons, had crews of up to 25 men and, with their three diesel engines, could attain speeds of between 36 and 40 knots. They carried two fixed torpedo tubes as well as 20 mm and later 40 mm quick-firing guns—the latter for protection against the increasingly formidable fighter-bomber attacks.

The rigours of operational service marked the features of those who manned the motor torpedo boats. About 250 of these E-boats were built, their bridges being armoured after 1943 against fire from low-flying aircraft. Their 11 flotillas were represented at all the focal points of the action off the coasts of Europe— from the North Sea to the Aegean and the Black Sea. Yet their main effort was in the Channel. In port they, like the U-boats, sheltered in concrete pens.

Biscay Operations

In an Atlantic coast base German torpedo boats await nightfall before steaming out into the Channel to lay mines under cover of darkness. The 1935–37 class torpedo boats, like the one on the right, with balloon, carried a 4-inch gun aft and could reach 34·5 knots. The 'fleet' torpedo boats, like *T30* below, displaced 1,294 tons, were armed with four 4-inch guns and could reach 32·5 knots. They were multi-purpose ships which could also be used as escort destroyers. They carried out many and varied duties in the Bay of Biscay.

Torpedo boats on convoy escort duty off France's Atlantic coast. The balloons moored to the ships act as a deterrent against low-flying aircraft. The boats also escorted blockade breakers from overseas into the Biscay ports—and often engaged British light forces.

The *Narvik* class Destroyers

These were the largest destroyers in the Second World War. They also carried 5.9-inch guns whereas English and American destroyers had only 4.7- or 5-inch guns. Till now questions have been raised about their theoretical superiority, particularly in the light of the fact that they achieved no noteworthy successes. As is so often the case, the practice did not live up to the theory: the 5.9-inch guns themselves raised problems.

In previous types of destroyers the weight of the two single 5-inch guns installed forward was 20.4 tons. It was a known fact that these boats dipped their bows deep into the sea because of the weight, and that in a following sea, because of the weight forward, they yawed badly and were hard to handle. The destroyer commanders therefore suggested that two guns be mounted in a single turret, hoping that this would save weight. In fact the combined weight of the twin 5.9-inch guns and their so-called 'C36 lightweight turret' was 60.4 tons, nearly three times the weight of the previous guns.

'Those at the front would be pleased', wrote the S.O. *Narvik* destroyer flotilla Captain Hans Erdmenger in a critical report to the naval high command, 'to know why our twin turrets weigh so very much more than those of other navies.' For a long time the world's leading navies had installed 4.7-inch and 5-inch twin turrets on destroyers; the British *Tribal* class for example, of 1,870 tons, carried eight 4.7-inch guns in four twin turrets, each turret weighing only around 25 tons. Added to this drawback in the *Narvik* class destroyers was the severe physical strain of loading the guns, which had to be done by hand—and each shell weighed 100 lb. As Erdmenger put it, 'the strength of our sailors is not such that they can load a shell weighing nearly a hundredweight without difficulty'.

The biggest and strongest destroyers of the period were built during the war in German yards. They were officially designated type 1936A (Mob) but in the Navy they were named *Narvik* class after the ten destroyers sunk at Narvik. The picture below shows *Z34*, 2,603 tons. With five 5.9-inch guns, these ships were, for destroyers, exceptionally heavily armed.

The 5.9-inch twin turret on the forecastle—here on *Z39*—was the distinguishing mark of the *Narvik* destroyers. The weight of the turret adversely affected the sea-keeping qualities and manoeuvrability in heavy seas. As on all German destroyers, the torpedo armament consisted of two sets of four swivel-mounted tubes.

The Senior Officer of the 8th destroyer flotilla, Captain Hans Erdmenger, steamed out into the Bay of Biscay on Christmas Eve 1943, with six destroyers and six torpedo boats, in order to meet and escort back to the Gironde a single ship, the blockade-runner *Osorno*, laden with valuable raw materials from the Far East. The operation was partly successful, all air attacks being beaten off, but in the Gironde estuary the *Osorno* ran on to a wreck and had to be beached to save the cargo.

Two days later the operation was repeated, this time with the blockade-runner *Alsterufer*, but the ship had already been hit by bombs before the warships reached it. In a storm the destroyers and torpedo boats encountered the British cruisers *Enterprise* and *Glasgow*, and after a fierce gun battle the German destroyer *Z27*, with the flotilla Senior Officer on board, and the torpedo boats *T25* and *T26* (left), sank. In spite of numerical superiority the German boats were very difficult to handle in the bad weather and heavy seas, and were no match for the British guns.

The longer the war lasted, the more destructive became Allied air power, and the Luftwaffe became incapable of bringing relief to shipping under attack. The ships gave of their best, but Allied air power was overwhelming. The picture below shows the flak-ship *Arcona*, a converted light cruiser.

An air attack on the German destroyer *Z24* (background) and the fleet torpedo boat *T24* off Le Verdon on the Gironde estuary. At the start of the Normandy invasion both boats had tried to press home an attack on the landing fleet but in a night action had been driven off by British destroyers. Here is depicted their destruction from the air on 24–25 August 1944.

A *Narvik* class destroyer returns to its French base after a tough fight in the Bay of Biscay.

Opposite, top: many ships of foreign navies sailed under the German flag after being commandeered in captured harbours and shipyards.

Opposite, middle: the 738-ton torpedo boat *TA29*, formerly the Italian *Eridano*, at Genoa. She was sunk in action in March 1945.

Opposite, bottom: the Scottish-built Yugoslavian destroyer *Dubrovnik*, 1,850 tons and armed with four 4.1-inch guns, sailed under the German flag as *TA32* from July 1944.

The 'Fleet in Being'

At the outset the Supreme Commander's fear was of an imaginary threat: Hitler took seriously the rumours widespread around the turn of 1941–42 that forcast an imminent Allied landing in Norway. What mattered to the enemy was 'that Russia's resistance should be sustained by vast supplies of war materials and food and that a second front in Europe should thus be established'—this was stated in a directive from the Führer on 14 March 1942. It went on: 'the regular and considerable convoy traffic from Scotland to Murmansk and Archangel can serve both purposes. We must reckon on the Allies landing on the Arctic coast . . .' In the face of direct opposition from the naval high command, which in spite of severe set-backs was still determined to continue the war in the Atlantic with the big ships, Hitler had already by this time put in hand the withdrawal of the big ships from the Atlantic bases in order to establish a new strongpoint on Europe's threatened northern flank.

Trondheim, Bogenbucht near Narvik and Altafjord were now turned into German naval bases. The moment seemed near when a strong German battle fleet, supported by Goering's bomber squadrons flying from north Norway, would make the Arctic an uncomfortable place for the Allies. This force was to consist of the battleships *Tirpitz* and *Scharnhorst*, the carrier *Graf Zeppelin*, whose halted construction was now resumed, the heavy cruisers *Hipper*, *Lützow* and *Scheer*, and last but not least two or

The heavy cruiser *Admiral Scheer* which at the end of 1941 the Naval Staff had intended to employ once more as a raider on the high seas, but which was kept back in Norway on Hitler's orders.

Germany's 'fleet in being' lay in the fjords of Norway. Here the heavy cruiser *Admiral Hipper* is steaming to her anchorage with a destroyer escort.

The picture on the left shows Grand Admiral Raeder on board the battleship *Tirpitz*, lying ready at Trondheim but scarcely able to move owing to fuel shortage. Behind Raeder are the Commander-in-Chief of the fleet, Admiral Schiewind and Vice Admiral Kummetz.

Even in the fjords the British made every effort to cripple the German ships from the air. The picture shows *Admiral Scheer*, camouflaged against aerial attack, firing her AA guns.

three destroyer flotillas which could put twelve to fourteen ships into action against the enemy.

The fact that these plans stuck halfway and that these ships never performed a combined operation was partly due to fuel shortage, which by 1942 was severe, and partly to Hitler's fear of the risk involved: he would agree to the heavy ships putting to sea only when the enemy was out of range and his ships were in no danger.

Nevertheless, in strategical terms, it is clear that the mere presence of this fleet, even though it was tied up in harbour, exercised pressure on the enemy and influenced his actions. Proof of this was furnished by the British Admiralty with their precipitate, even confused orders to convoy PQ17, which would never have dispersed and subsequently been destroyed by German U-boats and aircraft if an attack by the German surface fleet had not seemed to be a real threat. In fact the German fleet, through fear of a direct engagement with British battleships and carriers, was held back hour after hour and finally made only a feint sortie. Afterwards the British concentrated on ferreting out the German ships in their lairs, on attacking them, and on eliminating them from the struggle—with a good deal of success, as we shall see.

After the convoy PQ17 catastrophe, PQ18, steaming through the Arctic in September 1942, was also attacked by U-boats and aircraft and suffered losses. Once again the German fleet was not allowed to attack in case it came up against equally powerful Allied ships.

On the left is a rare picture showing the mighty *Tirpitz* on one of her few sorties during which Spitzbergen was bombarded. Two weeks later, on 22 September 1943, British midget submarines penetrated to the battleship's anchorage and did severe damage to her, leaving only *Scharnhorst* operational.

Tragedy off the North Cape

Scharnhorst on the way to northern Norway. She was to have been paid off on 1 July 1943, but the new Commander-in-Chief of the Navy, Grand Admiral Dönitz, carried through her transfer to No. 1 Task Force. The picture on the right shows the two triple 11-inch turrets on the iced-up deck.

On New Year's Eve 1942 a German task force, consisting of the heavy cruisers *Hipper* and *Lützow* and six destroyers, attacked an Allied Arctic convoy. In spite of favourable conditions and a theoretically perfect plan of attack, operation Rainbow miscarried completely. Blizzards, half-light and a resolute British escort force hindered the Germans from penetrating to the freighters, fully laden with war materials for Russia. Thus, failure took the place of the expected success—and the German group suffered damage and losses to boot.

This mishap led to a dramatic change of leadership in the German Navy. Hitler, completely disillusioned by the uselessness of the big ships, ordered that the fleet be paid off and broken up. Grand Admiral Raeder protested bitterly at this decision, which would give the British 'the cheapest victory in their history', and, as his words had no effect, handed in his resignation. The man named as his successor and also as Grand Admiral was U-boat chief Karl Dönitz, who now saw the achievement of his aims in sight: at last all the capacity of the German shipyards could be channelled into the building of U-boats and their repair. On 8 February 1943 the plan for the withdrawal of the big ships was presented, but by 26 February Dönitz had changed his mind. He persuaded Hitler that the battleship *Scharnhorst* be sent to north Norway to strengthen the German battle group. 'In view of the intensive campaign on the Eastern front', Dönitz claimed, 'I consider it my duty to put the ships into action.' Hitler remained sceptical, but he let his new chief of the Navy have his own way.

Even on the battleships, the deck, guns and superstructure iced up in heavy seas in the polar winter. The picture above shows a starboard 5.9-inch twin turret completely coated with ice. On the right, above, is the Senior Officer destroyers, Rear Admiral Erich Bey, under whose command *Scharnhorst* made her last fateful journey at Christmas 1943.

Thus 1943 too saw a German battle group in Altafjord, but a group now freed by its new master of the constraints imposed by Hitler's fears for its safety. It was to carry out a full-blooded attack as soon as a favourable opportunity presented itself, but no opportunity did. Smarting from the catastrophe of convoy PQ17 in summer 1942, the Allies sent no further supply convoys through the Arctic in the bright summer months. Instead, on 22 September 1943, they attempted to knock out the two German battleships at their anchorage with midget submarines. In the event the *Tirpitz* was badly damaged and was non-operational for six months. This left only the *Scharnhorst* as potential attacker of Arctic convoys, but the arrival of the polar winter reduced chances of success and no operations were planned.

However, a German weather aircraft sighted a Russia-bound convoy on 22 December 1943, and on Christmas afternoon the battle group received orders to attack. As justification for this decision the naval high command pointed to the situation on the Eastern Front. Seaborne supplies were absolutely vital to the Russians. The *Scharnhorst* and its five destroyers were to attack 'as soon as conditions permit'. Conditions in the polar night, of which the struggle in the Barents Sea less than a year before had left unhappy memories, were this time worsened by a raging south-westerly gale, which almost completely prevented the destroyers from using their armaments. Left on its own, the *Scharnhorst* opened fire twice on Boxing Day, at 09.26 and 12.24, on the convoy's cruiser covering force. Although their firepower was inferior, the British had the advantage, in the appalling visibility, of longer-range radar apparatus, which gave them better information on the enemy's movements. This led the German commander, Rear Admiral Erich Bay, wrongly to assume that his ship was being attacked by a powerful British force. In accordance with his orders, he turned about and steamed for the Norwegian coast, but on the way the *Scharnhorst* came directly under the guns of the 38,000-ton battleship *Duke of York*. The battle that ensued lasted three hours. Hit by heavy shells and numerous torpedoes, the *Scharnhorst* sank at about 19.45 off the North Cape, taking with her to the bottom 1,932 men. Only 36 were saved.

Chief adversary of *Scharnhorst* (bottom) in the battle off the North Cape was the flagship of the British Home Fleet, the 38,000-ton *Duke of York* (left) under Admiral Sir Bruce Fraser. This ship had been commissioned in November 1941 and carried ten 14-inch guns in two quadruple turrets and a single twin turret. But what gave her an advantage over *Scharnhorst* beyond simple gunnery superiority was her radar, which made a decisive difference in the polar winter.

The 5,042-ton Woermann motor-vessel *Togo* was, under the name 'Ship 14' *Coronel*, the last German auxiliary cruiser to try to break through the Channel in February 1943. Bomb hits forced her to turn back. Later she was converted into a nightfighter control ship for the Luftwaffe, as the picture (right) shows.

Even the Luftwaffe sometimes went by sea: these ferries, powered by twin BMW aero-engines, were used as transports on inland waters and would have been part of the invasion fleet. They carried anti-aircraft guns to protect them against attacks from the air.

The longer the war lasted, the greater became the danger from mines in coastal waters. Thousands of mines broke their mooring cables and had to be rendered harmless, whether they were threatening shipping or had been washed ashore.

More than two hundred mine clearance vessels were commissioned during the war to guide valuable ships through mine-invested waters.

Beaufighters attacking German mine-sweepers and patrol boats. In 1944 the Allied air superiority over the French Channel and Atlantic coasts was undisputed, a severe handicap for every German naval operation, at least by daylight.

In the early morning of 6 June 1944 began Operation Neptune, the biggest landing operation in the European war theatre, and the opening move in the Allied invasion of Normandy. The invasion fleet was supported by seven battleships, 23 cruisers, over 100 destroyers, and more than 1000 other fighting ships, together with thousands of aircraft.

The biggest German warships in the immediate area were five torpedo boats, which steamed out of Le Havre to meet the armada. Three flotillas of motor torpedo boats attacked at the same time and were able to sink a few landing craft, but the German destroyers coming from the Biscay ports were intercepted before reaching the area, and the U-boats too were unable to penetrate the armada's defences. These pictures show Allied landing craft off the coast and one of the artificial 'Mulberry' harbours, through which stores and reinforcements were pouring as soon as the attacking troops had set foot on the French shore.

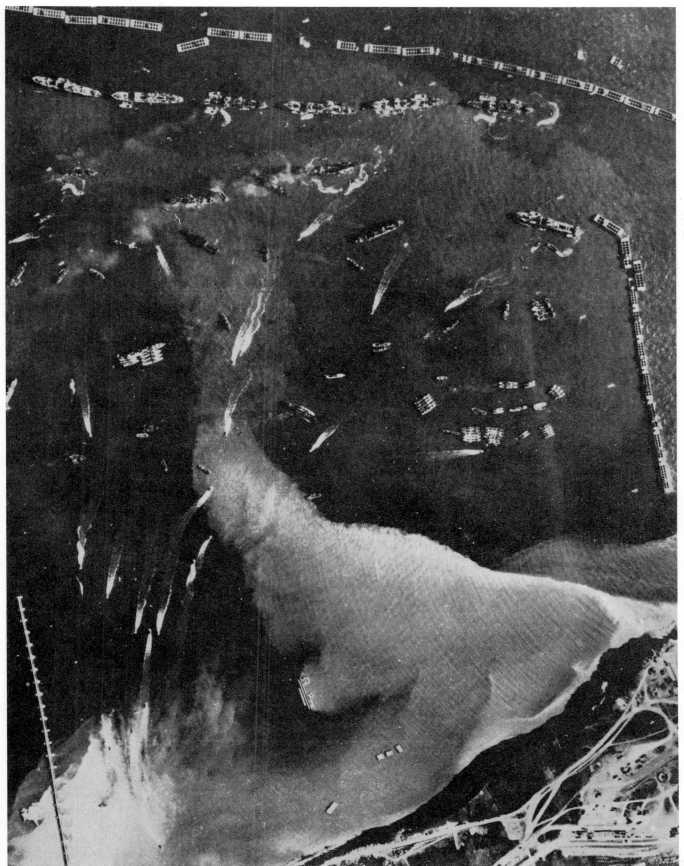

181

The Last Bid

From 1943, the *K-Verband* trained solo operators who distinguished themselves in various daring escapades. The *K-Verband*, or small battle units force, numbered in its ranks frogmen who operated in rivers behind the enemy lines, and one-man torpedoes (top picture). After firing the lower, live torpedo the operator returned to base in the upper, carrier torpedo. The *K-Verband* also used radio-controlled explosive motor-boats. The operator would leap out of the boat and be picked up by a control boat which would guide the explosive boat to its target. Both one-man torpedoes and explosive boats made successful surprise attacks on the invasion front in the Seine Bay.

One-man submarines of the *Biber* type being carried on the deck of a big U-boat to their operations zone. The attack planned for January 1945 by six *Biber* submarines of K-Flotilla 265 against shipping in Murmansk roads had to be called off when it was discovered that while lashed to the upperdeck of the U-boat, the vibration they had to endure opened up watertight joints and fractured petrol feed-pipes.

K-Flotilla 261 sailed from Rotterdam in the winter of 1944–45 against Allied supply shipping in the Schelde. The picture shows one of the operators checking his cooling-water valve before leaving. The biggest drawback of these tiny boats was their petrol engines, whose poisonous fumes often leaked into the cockpit.

The Destruction of the *Tirpitz*

Germany's biggest battleship, 'the lonely queen of the north', was no longer even safe in the fjords in 1944. On the right is a British photograph of *Tirpitz* at her last anchorage at Tromsö.

After the sinking of the *Scharnhorst* at Christmas 1943 off the North Cape the *Tirpitz* was the only German capital ship left in Norway to threaten Allied supplies passing through the Arctic. Yet the *Tirpitz* had only just finished repairs to the damage inflicted by the mines planted five months before by British midget submarines, and had just begun sailing trials, when trouble came her way again. The British Home Fleet, with two battle-ships, six carriers and many cruisers and destroyers, was in the area once more, escorting the 49 fully-laden ships of convoy JW.58. The *Tirpitz* obviously did not go out to meet this superior force, but the enemy came right up to her hiding place and attacked. On 3 April 1944, 40 dive bombers from the carriers, and as many fighters, were over Altafjord. *Tirpitz* was hit by 14 bombs, suffered severe losses of men and was once more knocked *hors de combat.*

From now on this mighty battleship, which had never fought a naval action had to fight for her life. Her enemies gave her no time to be repaired. Four more attacks by carrier-borne aircraft in August failed to hit home hard enough, and the British stepped up their effort by sending in four-engined Lancaster bombers. When these made their first attack on 15 September a special 5.4-ton bomb struck the *Tirpitz* forward. There was no question of effecting a repair so far from home, and the *Tirpitz* was towed to Sandesund near Tromsö, to serve there as a floating battery. It was here, on 12 November 1944, that she met her end. After suffering numerous direct hits she capsized, losing 902 sailors who were unable to get out of the capsized wreck.

The finale. The pictures show (left) super-heavy 12,000-lb. 'Tallboy' bombs exploding on and around *Tirpitz* and (above) the crater made by a bomb that missed. The frequent attacks by the Royal Navy had certainly crippled *Tirpitz*, but it was R.A.F. Bomber Command that dealt the final blow.

The new generation of U-boats differed markedly from their predecessors in appearance. The Type XXI (above) and the smaller Type XXII (right) were the first true submarines. Bigger batteries and more powerful electric motors enabled them to travel faster underwater than a convoy on the surface. This removed one of the previous U-boats' most severe disadvantages: having to operate on the surface after only a short period underwater.

The New U-boats

From the beginning, before the war, U-boat chief Karl Dönitz had expressed his concern that U-boats would soon be compelled by aircraft to remain submerged, where they were slow-moving and could carry out their battle duties only with difficulty. A solution was offered by the power unit being developed by Professor Walter, which used hydrogen peroxide to generate oxygen for its engines. This U-boat was therefore not dependent on supplies of fresh air, and was capable of high speeds underwater, but its trials had not been completed when the failure of the U-boat campaign in early 1943 revealed the weaknesses of the submarines then in use. As an interim solution the Navy built 'electro-boats', which were faster underwater, having double the normal battery capacity. 119 of the big Type XXI boats and 62 of the smaller Type XXII had been completed, despite bombing raids, by the end of the war, but only a few reached the operational stage, and, in any case, by 1943 the outcome of the battle of the Atlantic had been decided.

Ready for action in Bergen: the war ended before the first fully worked-up Type XXI boats could be sent out on their first patrols. They displaced 1,623 tons and were equipped with the most modern apparatus, including underwater acoustic location equipment. Their torpedoes were fired from six bow tubes. These boats too could be surprised on the surface by enemy aircraft and sunk, like the one pictured on the left, attacked *en route* to Norway.

U793, a prototype fitted with Walter turbines, on trials in Hamburg harbour. This development was not ready for operational use during the war and was soon rendered obsolete after the war by the adoption of atomic power for submersible craft.

Flight across the Baltic

Naval bombardment was used on the Baltic coast in the defensive battle raging inland. The picture shows the heavy cruiser *Prinz Eugen*, which has rammed the light cruiser *Leipzig* amidships. This happened in fog in the Gulf of Danzig on 15 October 1944. It took 14 hours to separate them and tow them into port.

From January to May 1945, in the last months of the war, the German Navy was called to carry out a big operation—the biggest rescue operation in history. The Red Army had cut off East Prussia, and later Pomerania and West Prussia, from the rest of the Reich. Soon there remained only one possible chance for hundreds of thousands of people to escape to the West: by fleeing over the Baltic. All warships and merchant ships still seaworthy—all which had no important military purpose to fulfil and had enough fuel in their bunkers—were sent across the Baltic to points of embarkation on the Gulf of Danzig. As the rescue operation progressed, and more and more refugees, wounded, and eventually fighting troops, were shipped out, it became clear that it was the biggest job the Navy had undertaken in the five and a half years of the war. In spite of severe losses from Soviet air attacks, mines and submarines, which sank many fully laden ships, the success of the operation is undisputed today. More than two million men, women and children who embarked in the midst of the chaos of the German collapse reached the West by sea, and what the beaten Navy did for them will never be forgotten.

Converted coasters like the 'heavy artillery carrier' *Nienburg* shown here formed part of the Navy's forces in the final battle on the Baltic. The main task was to carry back to Germany refugees and soldiers, and every available vessel was pressed into service. The middle picture shows a transport in the Gulf of Danzig; the bottom picture, troops aboard the destroyer *Z34*.

10 May 1945. The motor torpedo boats' crews parade for the last time on their boats to lower the flag. The sailors carried out their duties right to the very end.

One of the Allies' stipulations was that the entire German fleet should be handed over to them. The naval high command gave orders that nothing should be sunk or destroyed, but many U-boats were scuttled by their crews. The harbours and coasts gave a clear picture of the destruction.

Index

Figures in italics refer to illustrations